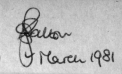

1 Corinthians

A Digest of Reformed Comment

1 Corinthians

A Digest of Reformed Comment

GEOFFREY B. WILSON
MINISTER OF BIRKBY BAPTIST CHURCH
HUDDERSFIELD

THE BANNER OF TRUTH TRUST

THE BANNER OF TRUTH TRUST
3 Murrayfield Road, Edinburgh EH12 6EL
P.O. Box 621, Carlisle, Pennsylvania, 17013, USA

*

© Geoffrey Backhouse Wilson 1978
First published 1978
ISBN 0 85151 277 1

*

Set in 11 on 12 pt Bembo
Printed in Great Britain by
Hazell Watson & Viney Ltd
Aylesbury, Bucks

TO MY WIFE
WITHOUT WHOSE HELP
THIS BOOK COULD NOT HAVE BEEN
WRITTEN

CONTENTS

PREFACE

The kind reception which was given to the first edition of this book encourages me to hope that it will prove even more useful in its revised form. This follows the text of the American Standard Version (1901), published by Thomas Nelson Inc., and also includes Chapter Summaries.

I would again express my thanks to the publishers for permission to quote from their books; to the Rev. Professor C. K. Barrett for allowing me to make use of his work on this Epistle; and to the Rev. K. MacLeay of Beauly for the loan of a rare volume by Anthony Burgess.

Huddersfield,   GEOFFREY B. WILSON
January 1978

INTRODUCTION

After the destruction of the old city of Corinth in 146 BC by the Romans under Lucius Mummius, the site remained unoccupied until a century later when it was refounded as a Roman colony by Julius Caesar. New Corinth soon became an important political and commercial centre with a large cosmopolitan population. Unfortunately the revival of its civic eminence was marred by the same vices which in former days had made its name a byword for immorality even in the ancient world.

Paul came to Corinth about AD 51. The opposition and indifference which he had encountered in Macedonia and Athens were not calculated to inspire the hope that his reception in Corinth would be any more favourable to the gospel, but encouraged by the Lord in a vision he persevered in the work for eighteen months [*Acts* 18:1–18]. Although the church thus founded was the crowning achievement of the second missionary journey, its further advance was hindered by troubles which almost overwhelmed him with grief.

It appears from 1 *Cor* 5:9 that while Paul was at Ephesus he had occasion to reprove the Corinthians for their moral laxity in a 'previous' letter which has not been preserved. Some time later 'Chloe's people' brought disturbing news of divisions within the church [1:11], and he also received an official letter asking for guidance on particular matters of faith and practice (note the repeated 'now concerning': 7:1; 7:25; 8:1; 12:1; 16:1; 16:12). It may well be that Paul wrote this Epistle over a period of several weeks, dealing first with the emotive issues raised by what had been told him of the state of the church [ch 1–6], and then replying to the questions put to him by the Corinthians in their letter [ch 7ff].

Whether or not this letter was delivered by the church leaders mentioned in 1 Cor 16:17, their welcome visit doubt-less supplied him with additional information on the problems they were facing. The Epistle that is known to us as 'First' Corinthians was the Apostle's inspired reply to the varied demands of this dangerous situation. It was in bringing the light of the cross to bear upon a great diversity of subjects that Paul attained a marvellous unity in his letter, and showed the only way in which harmony could be restored at Corinth. The unique authority of the deliverance assures the people of God in every age that a consistent application of the same gospel principles which were first laid down for them by a 'wise masterbuilder' is fully adequate to deal with every difficulty that would arrest their progress in the Christian Way.

CHAPTER ONE

In greeting the church at Corinth, Paul reminds this community of his own calling as an apostle, and of their call to be saints. He thanks God for their rich spiritual endowments, and encourages them with the assurance that God will keep them to the end [vv 1–9]. Paul begins by appealing for unity, for he has heard that their fellowship is fractured by party strife. As these sinful divisions were caused by the folly of glorying in men, Paul is glad that he had baptized so few of them personally, because this showed he could not be charged with having baptized in his own name [vv 10–16]. For Christ had not sent Paul to baptize, but to preach the unadorned word of the cross. And though the wisdom of the world rejects this message as foolishness, believers have found it to be the power and the wisdom of God. Hence the Corinthians must not glory in that wisdom which was confounded by God in their own calling. Thus the fact that they owe their salvation solely to the grace of God must teach them to glory only in the Lord [vv 17–31].

V1: **Paul, called *to be* an apostle of Jesus Christ through the will of God, and Sosthenes our brother,**

According to his usual practice, Paul invests the normal form of greeting with a distinctively Christian content which subtly prepares his readers for what is to follow it. Since Paul's authority is in dispute [9:1], he begins by reminding the

Corinthians that he is 'a called apostle'. Because his conversion coincided with this commission, he could never refer to the powers he exercised as an apostle without recalling that great watershed in his spiritual experience. Consequently the validity of his subsequent career rested entirely upon the reality of this encounter with the person of the exalted Christ [*Acts* 26:9–20]. Moreover, the eternal purpose of God for his life was revealed to him in the call of Christ [*Gal* 1:15, 16]. Thus Paul's right to command the obedience of the church in Corinth is based on the unshakeable conviction that he was appointed to this high office by the direct intervention of God.

and Sosthenes the brother, (ASV margin). It is impossible to say for certain whether this is the Sosthenes referred to in *Acts* 18:17. But whoever he was, it is clear that Paul is glad to associate himself with an honoured colleague who is evidently well known to the readers, and whose brotherly concern for them is witnessed by his wholehearted approval of the apostle's message, though he plainly had no part in its composition. For 'he did not stand in any position of authority, he has no special connexion with the contents of the Epistle, and does not reappear again directly or indirectly, but the Apostle at once returns to the singular, "I thank my God" [1:4], (J. B. Lightfoot). Ever since the Christian experience of forgiveness first brought a new wealth of meaning to the word 'brother', the sons of grace have been distinguished by their unfeigned love for the brethren [1 *Pet* 1:22; 1 *John* 3:14].

*V*2: **unto the church of God which is at Corinth,** *even* **them that are sanctified in Christ Jesus, called** *to be* **saints, with all that call upon the name of our Lord Jesus Christ in every place, their** *Lord* **and ours:**

Despite glaring imperfections which merited the sternest reproofs, Paul does not hesitate to address this group of people as 'the church of God which is at Corinth'. The word 'church' (*ekklēsia*) was originally used of any secular assembly (*e.g.* the Ephesian concourse, *Acts* 19:32, 39, 41), but Christians probably made it their own because it is used of 'the congregation' of Israel in the Greek version of the Old Testament [cf *Acts* 7:38 RSV]. As the word itself suggests, the church consists of those whom God has 'called out' from the world into fellowship with himself. But if God designs to separate his people from the world, the establishment of the church in pagan Corinth proves that it is not his will immediately to remove them from it [cf 5:10; *Matt* 5:14; *John* 17:15]. The apostle who had no wish to encourage the Corinthians to be unmindful of either the faith or the needs of other Christian communities, nevertheless recognized the existence of the church of God in all its fulness at Corinth. For wherever two or three are gathered together in Christ's name, he is truly present in the midst [*Matt* 18:20].

even them that are sanctified in Christ Jesus, cf 1:30. The church is further defined as consisting of those whom God has set apart for himself '*in* Christ Jesus'. The preposition shows that it is solely through the work of Christ that this consecration is initiated and sustained. 'The Corinthians are not born saints but they are sanctified by virtue of an act of God in Jesus, the consequences of which last till the present' (F. W. Grosheide).

called *to be* saints, The designation expresses the purpose for which they have been set apart by God. As Paul is a 'called apostle', so the Corinthians are 'called saints'. Unless 'sainthood' were first bestowed, it could never be acquired. But the ethical demand for holy living is inseparable from what is freely given in the gospel, and so it is the vocation of those who have been made saints by God to become in daily obedience what they are 'in Christ Jesus' [1 *Pet* 1:15]. There-

[15]

fore, to remind them of their calling is also to rebuke them for their sin.

with all that call upon the name of our Lord Jesus Christ in every place, Although what Paul has to say in this letter is addressed to the Corinthians, he wants to make them conscious of their spiritual kinship with all other believers wherever they may live. This is the true antidote for an insular faith. We are not to isolate ourselves from our fellow-believers, for we are members together with all the saints of God [14:36]. Matthew Poole rightly observes that this 'is an eminent place to prove the Divine nature of Christ; he is not only called *our Lord*, our common Lord, but he is made the object of invocation and Divine worship' so that 'none but such as call upon the name of Jesus Christ our Lord, are fit matter for a gospel church'. This of necessity excludes all who 'deny the Godhead of Christ' from any place in the church of God, whatever pretensions are made to the contrary [1 *John* 5:20; 2 *John* 7].

their *Lord* and ours: This afterthought corrects any possible misunderstanding of the word 'our'. For, adds Paul, he is not only *our* Lord but also *their* Lord! There is here 'a covert allusion to the divisions in the Corinthian church, and an implied exhortation to unity' (Lightfoot).

*V*3: **Grace to you and peace from God our Father and the Lord Jesus Christ.**

Grace to you and peace The appearance of this phrase throughout the New Testament suggests that it was the common form of greeting among Christians, and the 'password' by which they recognized one another. The order of the words is always the same, for without an experience of the grace of God there can be no knowledge of the peace of God. But to enjoy the unmerited favour of God in Jesus

Christ is to be made a partaker of that peace which ensures the spiritual prosperity of the whole man.

from God our Father and the Lord Jesus Christ. These blessings flow down to men from above. The linking together here of 'God' and 'Lord' under a common preposition ('from') is an indication of their essential equality. This disclosure of Paul's attitude toward Christ is all the more impressive because it is incidentally revealed rather than formally defined.

*V*4. **I thank my God always concerning you, for the grace of God which was given you in Christ Jesus;**

As in secular correspondence the greeting is followed by the thanksgiving, though in Paul's Epistles the form is never used to win the readers' goodwill but rather to thank God for their faith (with the exception of Galatians where the apostle saw no such cause for thanksgiving, cf *Gal* 1:6). Since Paul is here referring to his prayers for the Corinthians, it is quite wrong to suggest that this thanksgiving is tinged with irony, for at the outset of a letter filled with rebuke, he is at pains to assure them that the very existence of the church in a place like Corinth calls for constant thanksgiving to God.

Because the apostle delights to extol the grace of God in its essential character as an absolute grant to the undeserving, he underlines the fact that this was given them 'in Christ Jesus'. This objective salvation which is theirs in Christ is the basis upon which all the other spiritual graces and gifts that he enumerates are bestowed [*vv* 5–7].

*V*5: **that in everything ye were enriched in him, in all utterance and all knowledge;**

The Corinthians have been made rich by the grace of God, so that they abound '*in* all utterance and all knowledge'. The use of a single preposition shows that this spiritual wealth consisted in a thorough understanding of the gospel together with the power to give it eloquent expression. It is significant that Paul singles out the gifts upon which they set the greatest store. Yet he can no more refrain from rejoicing in these lavish endowments of God's grace than from censuring the Corinthians – and most justly so – for their sinful abuse of them [8:1ff; 12:8; 13:1ff].

V6: even as the testimony of Christ was confirmed in you:

This enrichment resulted from the spiritual quickening which was produced in their hearts through the testimony which Paul had borne to Christ in their city. The truth of what the apostle declared *to* them was confirmed *in* them by the Holy Spirit. All preaching must rely for its success upon the Spirit's work in confirming the truth of the message in those who hear it, for eloquence without power is idle rhetoric [cf 2:4].

V7: so that ye come behind in no gift; waiting for the revelation of our Lord Jesus Christ;

The shower of spiritual blessings which followed the conversion of the Corinthians leads to the conclusion that they do not come short of any gift of grace. The reference must not be restricted to the special gifts that were exercised in Corinth, but rather includes all spiritual endowments.

Although all the early Christians lived in eager expectation of Christ's appearing, in Corinth this hope had been dimmed by a spirit of sinful complacency with present good [4:8], and the airing of doubts concerning the resurrection [15:12]. The Corinthians therefore needed to be reminded of the great end of their calling, for only those who are looking for the Lord's return will live as they ought for him [*Tit* 2:12, 13; 1 *John* 3:2, 3; 2 *Pet* 3:11, 12]. 'It is the character of Christians, that they wait for Christ's second coming; all our religion hath regard to that: we believe it and hope for it, and it is the business of our lives to prepare for it, if we are Christians indeed' (Matthew Henry).

*V*8: **who shall also confirm you unto the end,** *that ye be* **unreprovable in the day of our Lord Jesus Christ.**

'Who' refers to Christ [*v* 7], who acts on God's behalf. Christ has not only saved the Corinthians, but he will also keep them to the end. As the appointed judge of all men [*Rom* 2:16], Christ will then declare his people to be 'unreprovable' The word 'implies not merely acquittal, but the absence of even a charge or accusation against a person' (W. E. Vine). Yet now they are far from being beyond reproach, for the apostle is himself about to level grave charges against them. But they will be 'exempt from accusation' in the day of judgment [*Rom* 8:33; *Col* 1:22], because then their subjective state will perfectly correspond with the objective standing which is already theirs in Christ. Thus F. Godet remarks, 'If then they are no longer subject to any accusation, it will not be only, as during their earthly career, in virtue of their justification by faith, it will be in virtue of their thenceforth perfected sanctification'.

in the day of our Lord Jesus Christ. This affords another striking proof of the Deity of Christ. It is because God has revealed his purpose to judge the world by Jesus Christ that the Old Testament 'day of Jehovah' is now spoken of as the 'day of Christ'.

*V*9: **God is faithful, through whom ye were called into the fellowship of his Son Jesus Christ our Lord.**

Since God has called the Corinthians to salvation through Christ, his faithfulness is the guarantee that he has not called them in vain [10:13; *Phil* 1:6; 1 *Thess* 5:24]. The call that came to them through the preaching of the gospel is an effectual calling, because it took place in accordance with God's antecedent purpose of grace [*Acts* 18:10; *Rom* 8:30; 2 *Tim* 1:9]. It is by this creative intervention of God that they have been brought into fellowship with his Son. The meaning is not that they partake of the divine essence after the manner of the pagan mystery religions, but that their final glorification is certified by the faith-union which has made them present sharers in Christ's resurrection life (cf *Col* 3:4].

*V*10: **Now I beseech you, brethren, through the name of our Lord Jesus Christ, that ye all speak the same thing, and *that* there be no divisions among you; but *that* ye be perfected together in the same mind and in the same judgment.**

The apostle begins with an urgent appeal for unity. The adversative 'now' is in painful contrast with the thanksgiving, for the existence of factions within the church is a flagrant contradiction of that 'fellowship' to which the Corinthians were called by God [*v* 9]. The inconsistency of these divisions is also implied by the affectionate address 'brethren'.

through the name of our Lord Jesus Christ, In the first ten verses Christ's name occurs no less than ten times. This emphatic repetition is meant to remind them that the church belongs to Christ and not to men. Here the 'appeal to the one Name is an indirect condemnation of the various party-names' (Robertson – Plummer). [*v* 12].

that ye all speak the same thing, As the meaning of this classical expression is 'to make up differences' (Lightfoot), Paul is calling for something more than mere unanimity of utterance. But since there can be no such restoration of harmony unless all do say the same thing, the admonition obviously demands the abandonment of party slogans which can only foster strife within the church.

and *that* there be no divisions among you; Negatively, there must be an end to the cleavages which were caused by partisan preferences for individual leaders. For though the whole community still met together for worship [11:17ff], these internal 'dissensions' were threatening to tear it apart.

but *that* ye be perfected together in the same mind and in the same judgment. Positively, these breaches in the fellowship are to be healed. The order is experimental. Unity of judgment is not to be expected until they share the same frame of mind. 'He is urging them to give up, not erroneous beliefs, but party-spirit' (Robertson – Plummer).

*V*11: **For it hath been signified unto me concerning you, my brethren, by them *that are of the household* of Chloe, that there are contentions among you.**

Although the elders of the church did not see fit to mention these divisions in their letter to Paul, he had been informed of the seriousness of the situation by members of Chloe's household. They were probably slaves who had visited the apostle in Ephesus while on business for their mistress [*v* 26]. We do not know whether she was herself a Christian, but she was evidently known to the Corinthians.

*V*12: **Now this I mean, that each one of you saith, I am of Paul; and I of Apollos; and I of Cephas; and I of Christ.**

What Paul roundly condemns is the factious spirit which has led to the formation of these parties within the church; he gives no hint of any doctrinal deviation from the faith. Apollos may have been the unwitting cause of the trouble, for some in Corinth found his polished speech more to their taste than the plain preaching of Paul. Those who regarded this as a challenge to their loyalty to the apostle would be provoked to counter it with the cry, '*I* am of Paul'. Presumably Jewish believers were responsible for dismissing the rival claims of the Paul-party and the Apollos-party with the retort, 'But *I* am of Cephas'. It is unnecessary to assume that Peter had visited Corinth in order to account for the existence of this group. Finally, those who were disgusted with the unseemly conflict over personalities would say, 'I belong to *Christ*!' The apostle's total rejection of these opposing cliques is explained in chapter 3:22f. For the groups who chanted these slogans erred by showing a sinful partiality for the human leaders whom God had given for the benefit of the whole church. But as Paul's indignant rejoinder makes clear ('Is Christ divided?'), the error of those whose watchword made Christ their own private property was even more grievous.

*V*13: **Is Christ divided? was Paul crucified for you? or were ye baptized into the name of Paul?**

Moffatt renders the question, 'Has Christ been parcelled out?', and adds that 'though this protest covers all the groups, it starts from the sectional claim of the last-named clique'. In the second and third questions Paul in deference to the other leaders tactfully uses his own name to make the point. Since Paul was not crucified for the Corinthians and they were not baptized into his name, it is obvious that they do not belong to him but to Christ who bought them with his blood [6:20]. For when all Christ's members owe their salvation to his death for them, it is clear that no man can usurp the unique position which he now occupies as their exalted Lord [*Phil* 2:11]. In this indirect but forceful way the Corinthians are reminded that it was upon Christ's authority that they were baptized into his name, and so declared themselves to be his property [cf 3:23].

crucified . . . baptized 'The cross and baptism claim us for Christ. The correlatives are, redemption and self-dedication' (J. A. Bengel).

V14: I thank God that I baptized none of you, save Crispus and Gaius;

V15: lest any man should say that ye were baptized into my name.

In view of what had happened since he left Corinth, Paul regards it as a happy providence that *he* baptized so few while he was there. Crispus was the ruler of the synagogue where Paul began his mission [*Acts* 18:8], and Gaius is probably to be identified with Titus Justus who opened his house to the preaching of the gospel after the Jews had rejected it [*Acts* 18:7; *Rom* 16:23]. As a result, the Corinthians could neither say that they stood in any special relation to the apostle as their baptizer, nor deny the fact that they belonged to the Christ into whose name they had been baptized. 'The outrageous idea which Paul combats throughout is that men or any man should in any way be substituted for Christ in the church' (R. C. H. Lenski).

V16: And I baptized also the household of Stephanas: besides, I know not whether I baptized any other.

On second thoughts, Paul remembers or is perhaps reminded by his amanuensis that he also baptized the house of Stephanas, the first family in Achaia won to Christ. C. K. Barrett candidly concludes that though the meaning of 'household' cannot be decided with complete precision, 'it should be noted that at 16:15 *the household . . . of Stephanas* are said to *have set themselves for service to the saints*. This could hardly be said of children, and the presumption is that in using this word

CHAPTER I, VERSE 16

Paul is thinking of adults.[1]' On this temporary lapse of memory, Charles Hodge remarks that inspiration 'rendered its recipients infallible, but it did not render them omniscient. They were preserved from asserting error, but they were not enabled either to know or to remember all things.'

*V*17: **For Christ sent me not to baptize, but to preach the gospel: not in wisdom of words, lest the cross of Christ should be made void.**

That Paul had baptized so few in Corinth was not surprising: 'For Christ did not send me to baptize, but *to evangelize*' (G. G. Findlay). As an apostle it was not an essential part of his commission to baptize; his primary task was to make disciples through the preaching of the gospel [*Acts* 9:15. 22:14, 15; 1 *Tim* 2:7]. In consequence he usually delegated the baptizing to an assistant, and following Christ's own practice, it is likely that the other apostles did the same [*John* 4:1, 2; *Acts* 10:48]. 'Baptizing required no special, personal gifts, as preaching did. Baptism is not disparaged by this; but baptism presupposes that the great charge, to preach the gospel, has been fulfilled' (Robertson – Plummer). [*Matt* 28:19]

not in wisdom of words, Paul now begins to lay bare the root of the sinful divisions in the Corinthian church. The existence of these parties was not due to his activity in their midst, for he had been faithful both to the letter and the spirit of his commission. Not only did he evangelize without personally baptizing, but he also refused to embellish his message with 'cleverness in speaking' (Arndt-Gingrich). He confined himself to a simple proclamation of the facts of the gospel [15:1ff].

1. C. K. Barrett, *The First Epistle to the Corinthians*, p. 48, A. & C. Black.

lest the cross of Christ should be made void. The apostle had shunned this style of speech lest the cross of Christ should be emptied of its real significance. For though a dazzling display of rhetoric might impress the intellect, it would not lead the conscience to appropriate a divine salvation. 'The nucleus of the apostolic preaching was *a fact* – Christ crucified. To preach it as a philosophic system would be to empty it of its saving power, a truth which finds abundant and lamentable illustration in the history of the Church' (M. R. Vincent).

*V*18: **For the word of the cross is to them that perish foolishness; but unto us who are saved it is the power of God.**

Paul here exhibits 'the utter folly of trying to improve the word of the cross by casting it into the word of human wisdom in order to get rid of its apparent "foolishness" for a certain class of people' (Lenski).

For the word of the cross is to them that are perishing foolishness; (ASV margin) Those who regard the message of a crucified Christ as foolishness are not merely in the process of perishing; they are 'the perishing', i.e. those whose perdition is certain, for 'the perfective force of the verb implies the completion of the process of destruction' (Vine). It is not only because the unbelieving are spiritually dead that they are on the way to eternal ruin [2 *Thess* 1:9]. They also sentence themselves to this future doom by rejecting the only word which could deliver them from their present condition.

but unto us who are being saved it is the power of God. (ASV margin) The 'word of the cross' divides mankind into two classes only, the saved and the lost [cf 2 *Cor* 2:15f]. That the apostle and his readers are, by the grace of God, among those who 'are being saved' is indicated by the word 'us'.

'In the language of the New Testament salvation is a thing of the past, a thing of the present, and a thing of the future . . . It is important to observe this, because we are thus taught that "salvation" involves a moral condition which must have begun already, though it will receive its final accomplishment hereafter' (Lightfoot). So those whom God has declared righteous are in the process of being made holy, and this increasing conformity to Christ will be perfected in their glorification [1 John 3:2f].

It would have been true to say that the message which the lost dismiss as 'foolishness' is in fact 'the wisdom of God' [vv 24, 30], but before ever men can admire the infinite wisdom of the gospel they must experience its saving power [Rom 1:16]. For nothing less than 'the power of God' could suffice to save those 'who were dead in trespasses and sins' [Eph 2:1]. 'But only that gospel is the power of God which proclaims that the cross was the propitiation for sin, the sole ground of pardon . . . let anything else be substituted for the cross, and preaching is denuded of its efficacy, and stripped of this power' (George Smeaton).

V19: **For it is written,**
   I will destroy the wisdom of the wise,
   And the discernment of the discerning will I bring
      to nought.

The quotation is from *Isaiah* 29:14. The prophet predicts that God will nullify the worldly wisdom of Judah's politicians who hoped to counter the threat of Assyrian aggression through an alliance with Egypt. As this lack of trust in God exposed the hollowness of his people's worship [v 13], God will act in such a marvellous way that the folly of their reliance upon human wisdom will be decisively demonstrated [v 14]. 'This "wisdom" of Hezekiah's advisers was exactly like that which was trying to magnify itself in Corinth.

It emanated, not from God, but from godless thinking. The "prudence" of their tricky scheming failed to take into account God's promise and his power and was thus fit only to be cast aside and to be utterly forgotten. Paul would have his readers conclude from this quotation that what God did with this kind of wisdom in the days of old he does with all wisdom of this kind: he will destroy it and bring it to nought' (Lenski).

*V*20: **Where is the wise? where is the scribe? where is the disputer of this world? hath not God made foolish the wisdom of the world?**

Where is the wise? The first question is drawn from *Isaiah* 19:12. Pharaoh's counsellors, for all their false pretensions to wisdom, could not foresee, much less frustrate the judgment of Jehovah upon Egypt. The quotation is apt because the Greeks also gloried in their wisdom, but God will clearly show the futility of every form of reasoning that fails to reckon with him.

where is the scribe? The second question alludes to *Isaiah* 33:18. After God's deliverance of his people from the Assyrian danger, men will ask in astonishment, 'What has become of the scribe who was to tabulate the tribute to be taken from a conquered nation?' He is nowhere to be seen! In a similar way the salvation of God has made foolish the vaunted learning of the Jewish scribes. 'Knowledge of the Scriptures does not help if it is not accompanied by a believing submission to the word of the cross, the wisdom of God' (Grosheide). [cf *John* 5:39]

where is the disputer of this age? (ASV margin) Paul now adds a question of his own. The third term 'disputer' would apply equally well to the dialectical subtlety of the Greek and to the legal casuistry of the Jew. Moreover, the construction indicates that 'disputer', 'scribe', and 'wise', are all 'of this age'. Consequently their wisdom cannot transcend it. It is a wisdom which belongs to a world-order that is perishing. 'It is the gospel alone which connects us with the era to come, and this gospel is the truth which all the wise of this world reject as long as they remain only worldly-wise' (Lenski).

hath not God made foolish the wisdom of the world? The world and God are opposed, because each regards the other's wisdom as folly [*vv* 18, 25]. But in the preaching of Christ crucified, God actually turned to foolishness all the imagined wisdom of the world [*vv* 21–25].

*V*21: **For seeing that in the wisdom of God the world through its wisdom knew not God, it was God's good pleasure through the foolishness of the preaching to save them that believe.**

It was in accordance with God's plan that the world failed to gain the knowledge of God by its own wisdom. For it was his eternal purpose to save sinners through the cross of Christ, and the fulfilment of this wise decree demonstrated the folly of what the world accounted wisdom. This wisdom is always self-frustrating because it is essentially hostile to God. Those blinded by sin make God in their own image, and so fail to see that the 'God' thus made is merely an expression of their self-love. Men are delivered from this fatal reliance upon their own wisdom only when they are brought to recognize that they must receive 'the reconciliation' which God in his wisdom has provided through Christ crucified. '"Through its (Greek) wisdom the world *knew not* God," as through its (Jewish) righteousness it *pleased not* God . . . The intellectual was as signal as the moral defeat; the followers of Plato were "shut up", along with those of Moses, "unto the

faith which should afterwards be revealed" [*Gal* 3:22f]'
(Findlay).

**it was God's good pleasure through the foolishness of
the thing preached to save them that believe.** (ASV
margin) What the world regards as foolishness is not simply
the act of preaching, but the content of the message thus
proclaimed. 'To announce as the Saviour of the world one
who died the vile death of a criminal on the cross seems,
indeed, to be the acme of foolishness. To expect that this
announcement will do what all the world with its mighty
effort of wisdom failed to do, namely, actually to lift man up
again into communion with God, only intensifies the impression of utter foolishness' (Lenski). But the rejection of the
word of the cross is not universal, because it is the good
pleasure of God to save those who 'believe'. The tense of the
verb shows that it is not enough to have once believed, for in
the New Testament it is only a living faith that saves [cf
John 3:36: 'He that *believeth* on the Son hath everlasting life'].

*V*22: **Seeing that Jews ask for signs, and Greeks seek
after wisdom;**

This verse explains why the world deems God's wisdom
to be foolishness. The national characteristics of both
races 'are hit off to perfection in the words "ask"
and "seek". To the Jews God has already spoken; and they,
from the proud eminence of their divinely sprung religion,
"demand" of all upstart religions their proofs and credentials
[cf *Matt* 12:38, 16:1; *John* 6:30]. The Greeks, on the other
hand, are seekers; and they seek, as they worship, they know
not what. They can only give it the general name of wisdom
or truth' (T. C. Edwards). The paradoxical result was that
those who were opposed in every other respect found
themselves united in their rejection of the preaching of Christ

crucified, for it neither satisfied the Jewish expectation of a carnal kingdom nor rewarded the Greek quest for a philosophical explanation of the universe. As it was then, so it is now. It is because the gospel contradicts the presuppositions which underlie both the religion and the reasoning of the unregenerate that the world still continues to despise it.

*V*23: **but we preach Christ crucified, unto Jews a stumblingblock, and unto Gentiles foolishness;**

If no message was less welcome, none was more needed than this! 'Christ crucified' expresses more than the mere fact of his crucifixion, for the perfect tense indicates 'the *permanent character* acquired by it, whereby he is now a Saviour [*Gal* 3 :1].' (A. R. Fausset). Since the Jews anticipated the advent of a victorious prince who would liberate them from the oppressor's yoke, nothing could have been more repugnant to them than the scandal of a *crucified* Messiah [*Deut* 21:23; *Gal* 3:13]. It was the doctrine on which they stumbled and fell [*Rom* 9:33; 1 *Pet* 2:8]. 'To Jews "the word of the cross" announced the shameful reversal of their most cherished hopes; to Greeks and Romans it offered for Saviour and Lord a man branded throughout the Empire as amongst the basest of criminals; it was "outrageous", and "absurd"' (Findlay).

*V*24: **but unto them that are called, both Jews and Greeks, Christ the power of God, and the wisdom of God.**

'But unto the called themselves' (ASV margin) stresses the contrast between those who receive the gospel and those who reject it. It is only the effectual calling of God which accounts for the difference between these two groups. The fact that some Jews and Greeks do 'believe' [*v* 21] the message of salvation is not explained by Paul in terms of their 'free-will'; he attributes their faith to nothing but the gracious initiative of God. 'The apostle exalts the divine act in salvation; he sees God's arm laying hold of certain individuals, drawing them from the midst of those nationalities, Jewish and Gentile, by the call of preaching; then, when they have believed, he sees the Christ preached and received, unveiling himself to them as containing exactly all that their country-men are seeking, but the opposite of which they think they see in him' (Godet). For the doctrine of the Cross was to the Jews a stumblingblock, and to the Gentiles foolishness [*v* 23].

Christ the power of God, and the wisdom of God. 'Crucified' is omitted here, because when the offence of the cross is overcome, 'Christ' is received not only in his cross, but also in the power of his resurrection life. God thus puts his people in possession of a 'salvation, which is at once the mightiest miracle in the guise of weakness and the highest wisdom in the guise of folly' (Edwards). The order of the words teaches us that before men can admire the wisdom of God in Christ, they must first experience the divine power of Christ in vanquishing their sins.

*V*25: **Because the foolishness of God is wiser than men; and the weakness of God is stronger than men.**

Literally, Paul speaks of 'the foolish thing' and 'the weak thing' of God. By using neuter adjectives he 'avoids ascribing the abstract qualities of foolishness and of weakness to God as though they were two of his actual attributes' (Lenski). The reference is to the apparent foolishness and weakness of a particular act of God, namely, the death of Christ [cf 2 *Cor* 13:4]. 'For it is surely a foolish and a weak thing to let God's own Son die miserably on the cross . . . And yet this foolish and this weak thing outranks and absolutely outdoes all the wisdom and all the power of men . . . If men were asked how God should proceed to save the world they would certainly

[31]

not say by sending his Son to the cross. Yet this is what God did, and, behold this act saves! So wise is this foolish thing, so powerful this weak thing' (Lenski).

*V*26: **For behold your calling, brethren, that not many wise after the flesh, not many mighty, not many noble,** *are called:*

That God is resolved to reduce the world's wisdom to foolishness is now confirmed by an appeal to their own experience of his grace. For in Corinth not many of those who were great by worldly standards had been effectually called by God to faith in Christ; a humbling thought which is softened by the affectionate address, 'brethren'. Nothing could more clearly demonstrate the folly of their infatuation with human wisdom than a consideration of the divine reversal it received in their own calling. Thus they must learn that 'the things which elevate man in the world, knowledge, influence, rank, are not the things which lead to God and salvation' (C. Hodge).

*V*27: **but God chose the foolish things of the world, that he might put to shame them that are wise; and God chose the weak things of the world, that he might put to shame the things that are strong;**

But God chose the foolish and the weak things of the world, so that the wise who pride themselves on their wisdom, and the strong who glory in their strength might be 'put to shame'. In this and the following verse Paul is emphasizing the *creative character* of God's electing grace. For though God has chosen the foolish and the weak, it is in order to make them truly wise and strong: wise with his wisdom, and strong in his strength. 'Facing the disdainful attitude of the world the church may be comforted to know that God himself has called and elected her. Therein the church bears the character of the crucified Christ [Is 42.1f, *Matt 21.42*, 1 *Pet 2.6f*]' (Grosheide).

*V*28: **and the base things of the world, and the things that are despised, did God choose, *yea* and the things that are not, that he might bring to nought the things that are:**

The Corinthian church was the living proof that God's love did not stop short at the foolish and the weak; it even extended to those whom the world despised as base, whether by birth ('not *many* noble' 1:26) or by behaviour ('And such *were* some of you . . .' 6:11). Paul is not simply carried away by rhetoric when he adds that God has chosen 'the things that are not, that he might bring to nought the things that are' [cf *Rom* 4:17]. His words are full of meaning, as his readers ought to be the first to acknowledge. 'When God set his plan in motion there was no church in Corinth, save in his intention; notwithstanding opposition (and its own weakness), it now existed. God's wisdom in the gospel had already been validated by its effect, and will in the end be completely vindicated by the totality of the new creation' (Barrett).

*V*29: **that no flesh should glory before God.**

'Glory not *before* him, but *in* him (Bengel). Here Paul turns to his aim, to warn them that the preachers in whom they gloried had no ground for glorying in themselves; so the hearers ought to glory not in them, but in the Lord [3:21; 4:6]' (Fausset).

*V*30: **But of him are ye in Christ Jesus, who was made unto us wisdom from God, and righteousness and sanctification, and redemption:**

Paul intends to leave the Corinthians in no doubt whatsoever that they owe their salvation entirely to God's act. It is all 'of him' that they are now 'in Christ Jesus'. Such a gratuitous salvation evidently excludes all boasting in the flesh [Rom 3:27].

who became to us wisdom from God, Everlasting wisdom belonged to the eternal Son [Prov 8:22–31], but he 'became' the wisdom of God 'to us' when he entered into our lot. For it is God's wisdom to provide righteousness, holiness, and redemption for destitute sinners through Christ crucified, and these three terms define the nature of this objective achievement.

that is to say, righteousness and sanctification and redemption.

1. This righteousness was secured by the perfect obedience which Christ rendered to God in life and death. He fulfilled the law of God in his life, and exhausted its penalty in his death [Rom 3:25, 26]. Now believers are thus 'righteous, not in themselves, but in Christ [cf 2 Cor 5:21]. Christ is not only their justification, but also the ever-abiding cause of their remaining justified; that is, he is their righteousness' (Edwards).

2. This almost has the same meaning as 'righteousness', for Paul refers to the *status* of holiness which God confers upon believers in Christ [cf 6:11], and not to the *process* of sanctification in which their co-operation is enlisted. 'We must go back to the Jewish worshippers, and the severe prohibition against coming before God if not purified according to the preparation of the sanctuary; for persons defiled were without access, and debarred from fellowship with Jehovah and other worshippers. But, when sprinkled by the blood of sacrifices, they were readmitted to the worship. They were then a holy people. The blood of sacrifice was their sole ground of access. Even so, by means of the one ever valid sacrifice of Calvary, sinners excluded on account of sin have

access in worship and boldness to approach a holy God. In
that sense Christ crucified was made of God to us sanctification'
(Smeaton).

3. Redemption 'is the first gift of Christ to be begun in us,
and the last to be brought to completion. For salvation begins
when we are extricated from the labyrinth of sin and death.
In the meantime however we sigh for the final resurrection
day, yearning for redemption, as it is put in *Romans* 8:23. But
if someone asks how Christ has been given to us for redemption, I reply that he made himself the price of redemption'
(Calvin).

*V*31: **that, according as it is written, He that glorieth,
let him glory in the Lord.**

The Corinthian church was torn by party strife because its
members were glorying in men. They were guilty of extolling
the human agents through whom they had received their
salvation instead of exulting in the divine Author of it
[3:21, 22]. Paul's free citation of *Jer* 9:23, 24 is therefore
especially apposite, since it not only reveals their duty but also
condemns their sin. They are to glory only 'in the Lord';
that is, in Christ 'the Lord of glory' [2:8]. In ascribing this
divine honour to Christ, the apostle again points to his
Deity.

CHAPTER TWO

Paul defends his ministry among the Corinthians by reminding them that they did not owe their conversion to his own powers of persuasion, but to the power of God in blessing the preaching of a crucified Christ to their hearts [vv 1–5]. Although he had repudiated the world's wisdom, he insists that his message is the true wisdom, for now God's once hidden purpose of grace is revealed in the gospel and received through the Spirit [vv 6–13]. But though this wisdom is foolishness to the natural man who has no capacity to discern it, the spiritual man is able to form a judgement about all things because believers have the mind of Christ [vv 14–16].

V1: **And I, brethren, when I came unto you, came not with excellency of speech or of wisdom, proclaiming to you the testimony of God.**

It was in accordance with this principle [1:31] that Paul had abstained from presenting his message in a manner which would have commended itself to human wisdom. He disdained any show of superiority in the form ('speech') or content ('wisdom') of his teaching. He neither varnished the gospel by elaborate language ('Corinthian words'), nor distorted it by philosophical subtlety. The simple fact that Paul 'came' to Corinth proved that the church he planted there was no spontaneous growth, but a supernatural work of grace. In their admiration for later teachers the Corinthians had forgotten that their believing was the consequence of his coming [*Rom* 10:14f].

came . . . proclaiming to you the testimony of God. As they very well know, this was Paul's policy from the moment of his arrival in Corinth [1:6]. This is the testimony 'which God gives and which has God as its contents. Paul holds a mandate from God and he speaks of no one else but God. God has revealed himself and the centre of this revelation is the work of Christ. To speak of God is to speak of Christ. Here is a complete surrender to God and a giving up of all that is human. All this is expressed in the contrast between *I* at the beginning and *God* at the end of the verse' (Grosheide).

V2: For I determined not to know anything among you, save Jesus Christ, and him crucified.

'Paul does not say that, when he came to Corinth, he adopted a new evangelistic approach, and there is no suggestion that he had accommodated his message of "Christ and him crucified" to his hearers at Athens and now regretted it' (N. B. Stonehouse, *Paul before the Areopagus*, p. 36). The reason why Paul recalls the character of his ministry among the Corinthians is that those who were now enamoured of human wisdom needed an urgent reminder of the content of the gospel they had professed to believe. 'The plea that our age demands certain modifications of the gospel captivates many today, and they do not decide as Paul did. Of course, they intend to lose nothing of the gospel but only to aid it in finding more ready and widespread acceptance among men. But such good intentions on our part reflect on the Lord's intentions, who originally made the gospel what it is' (Lenski).

Jesus Christ, and him crucified. 'Paul's only design in going to Corinth was to preach Christ; and Christ not as a teacher, or as an example, or as a perfect man, or as a new starting point in the development of the race – all this would be mere philosophy; but Christ *as crucified*, i.e. as dying for our sins. Christ as a propitiation was the burden of Paul's preaching. It has been well remarked that *Jesus Christ* refers to the person of Christ, and *him crucified*, to his work; which constitute the sum of the gospel' (Hodge).

V3: And I was with you in weakness, and in fear, and in much trembling.

This includes whatever contributed to his sense of weakness. Paul felt quite unequal to the magnitude of the task which faced him in Corinth. Everything seemed to militate against the success of his mission, and heightened his own feeling of personal and bodily weakness. Hence the Lord's timely encouragement of his hard-pressed servant was by no means superfluous [*Acts* 18:9, 10]. 'Each word is an advance upon the other. The sense of weakness produced fear. The fear betrayed itself in much trembling . . . The expression denotes the Apostle's nervous apprehension that he might not fulfil his ministry aright: i.e. fear and trembling in the sight of God rather than of man' (Lightfoot) [cf *Phil* 2:12].

V4: And my speech and my preaching were not in persuasive words of wisdom, but in demonstration of the Spirit and of power:

'Speech' (or 'word') harks back to 'the word of the cross' [1:18], i.e. the gospel, while 'preaching' is the apostle's proclamation of it. Thus in neither the substance of his message nor in the manner of its presentation did Paul resort to 'persuasive words of wisdom' to make it more palatable to the natural man. 'My' is emphatic; 'contrasting his message with the dogmas of philosophers, his method with theirs' (Edwards).

but in demonstration of the Spirit and of power: Instead he relied entirely upon the Spirit of God to provide an indisputable proof of this testimony within the hearts of men. As in 1 *Thess* 1:5, Paul's first reference to the Spirit in this Epistle is linked to the 'power' which attended his preaching of the gospel. It was the Spirit who demonstrated the truth of the message by convicting the hearers of their need of Christ. And because that power did not proceed from himself [*v* 3] but from God [*v* 18], the Corinthians have no cause to glory in men [cf 1:31].

*V*5: **that your faith should not stand in the wisdom of men, but in the power of God.**

'That' points to the purpose of God in so dispensing with the wisdom of men. For a faith that depends upon clever reasoning may be demolished by a more acute argument, but the faith which is produced by the power of God can never be overthrown. Hence 'faith' is more than a mere intellectual conviction of the truth. 'It is trust in God; and this saving trust grows out of the all-powerful activity of the Divine Spirit' (Edwards) [*v* 12; 2 *Cor* 4:6, 7].

*V*6: **We speak wisdom, however, among them that are fullgrown: yet a wisdom not of this world, nor of the rulers of this world, who are coming to nought:**

But though faith does not depend upon the wisdom of men [*v* 5], the Corinthians must not think that 'the word of the cross' [1:18] is devoid of wisdom, for in common with all true preachers of the gospel ('we') Paul speaks the highest wisdom. Some take the 'fullgrown' to be Christians of mature understanding as distinguished from the 'babes' of 3:1, but this view is not favoured by the context which contrasts 'the called' or converted with the unbelieving who reject the gospel as foolishness [1:23, 24]. When contrasted with the unsaved it is appropriate to refer to all believers as the 'perfected' or the 'mature' because they alone 'have reached Christ crucified as the goal' (Lenski).

Although many commentators argue that 'the rulers of this world' is a reference to demonic powers, the apostle would not have expected his readers to grasp such an idea without a word of explanation, and it is preferable to take his words in their natural meaning [Acts 3:17]. So these rulers 'are to be understood as great men according to the world's estimate of greatness', whether in *intellect* ('wise'), *power* ('mighty'), or *rank* ('noble') as in 1:26 (Lightfoot). 'The word "rulers" must not be taken of magistrates only, since Paul has in mind all those who set the pattern of this world, including the rulers in the sphere of science and art. Of all of them it holds true that they *are coming to nought*' (Grosheide).

V7: but we speak God's wisdom in a mystery, *even* the *wisdom* that hath been hidden, which God foreordained before the worlds unto our glory:

But the wisdom we speak is diametrically opposed to the spurious wisdom of the world [*vv* 5, 6]. For it is *God's* wisdom, and this wisdom has been fully manifested in the gospel. Since nothing but the gospel can enrich the Corinthians with all the riches of God, they must not continue to hanker after that wisdom which leads only to final and fatal impoverishment. When Paul speaks 'wisdom among the mature', he is not setting forth a secret doctrine different from that preached to beginners, but the same 'word of the cross' – for he knows nothing greater or higher [*Gal* 6:14] – in its inner meaning and larger implications (Findlay).

in a mystery, even the wisdom that hath been hidden.
'The Christian "mystery" according to Paul is not something
that is to be kept secret on principle, like the mysteries of
Eleusis, but it is something which, though it was formerly
hidden in the counsels of God, is now to be made known to
all. Some, it is true, may never be able to receive it. But that
which is necessary in order that it may be received is not
"gnosis" or an initiation. It is rather acceptance of a message
and the holy life that follows. "If you would know the deep
things of God," Paul says to the Corinthians, "then stop your
quarrelling." We find ourselves here in a circle of ideas quite
different from that of the mystery religions' (J. G. Machen,
The Origin of Paul's Religion, p. 273) [*Rom* 16:25, 26; *Eph*
3:3–6; *Col* 1:26].

which God foreordained before the ages (ASV margin)
'Before man was formed, before the first phosphor light of
his little wisdom began to glow, God's wisdom was complete,
God's decision was fixed as to the object and as to the result
of that wisdom' (Lenski).

unto our glory: Our eternal glory is thus the result of God's
eternal decree. 'The wisdom of the great men of the world
ends in their destruction; God's wisdom leads, not only to
our salvation, but to our glory' (Edwards). Moreover, those
who are destined to share in the glory of 'outward exaltation'
[*Rom* 8:17, 18] are none other than those who even now
enjoy the glory of 'inward enlightenment' [2 *Cor* 3:18]. For
as fellowship with God on earth is glory begun, so fellowship
with God in heaven is glory consummated [*Ps* 73:23–26].

*V*8: **which none of the rulers of this world hath known:
for had they known it, they would not have crucified
the Lord of glory:**

None of the rulers of this world knew God's wisdom. '"Had

[41]

they discerned, as they did not, they would not have crucified, as they did." It is manifest from this that the "rulers" are neither demons nor angels, but the rulers who took part in crucifying the Christ' (Robertson-Plummer).

crucified the Lord of glory. This shows that Paul regarded Jesus, even in the days of his flesh, as the 'Lord to whom glory belongs as his native right' (B. B. Warfield, *The Lord of Glory*, pp 223-224). The expression strongly contrasts the essential glory of the Lord with the shame of his suffering. 'We see that the person of Christ may be designated from his divine nature, when what is affirmed of him is true only of his human nature . . . Whatever is true either of the soul or body may be predicated of a man as a person; and whatever is true of either the divine or human nature of Christ may be predicated of Christ as a person. We need not hesitate therefore to say with Paul, the Lord of glory was crucified; or even, in accordance with the received text in *Acts* 20:28, "God purchased the church with his blood." The person who died was truly God, although the divine nature no more died than the soul of man does when the breath leaves his body' (Hodge).

*V*9: **but as it is written,**
Things which eye saw not, and ear heard not,
And *which* entered not into the heart of man,
Whatsoever things God prepared for them that love
him.

'Not only was God's wisdom unknown to the princes of this world, but those things in which it manifests itself are in their nature such that their inner meaning cannot be known without a revelation of the Spirit within' (Edwards). Here Paul freely selects certain scriptural expressions from *Isaiah* 64:4 and 65:17, which he arranges in an ascending scale in order to show the absolute necessity of a divine disclosure of this mystery. 'By combining the three terms *seeing*, *hearing*, and *entering into the heart*, the apostle wishes to designate the three means of natural knowledge: sight, or immediate experience; hearing, or knowledge by way of tradition; finally, the inspirations of the heart, the discoveries of the understanding proper. By none of these means can man reach the conception of the blessings which God has destined for him' (Godet). The Corinthians prided themselves on their spiritual knowledge, but Paul does not say that these inconceivable blessings have been prepared for those who know God, but rather for those who *love* him [cf 8:3]. 'Not *gnosis* but love is the touchstone of Christian maturity and spirituality' (Barrett).

*V*10: **But unto us God revealed** *them* **through the Spirit: for the Spirit searcheth all things, yea, the deep things of God.**

But in the goodness of God, what could never be discovered by human reason has been revealed to Christians by the Holy Spirit. 'Searcheth all things' expresses the 'intra-divine activity of the Holy Spirit' (Godet). Since his knowledge of God is infinite, the fathomless depths of God hold no mysteries for him. And it is because he alone 'fathoms everything' (Arndt-Gingrich) that only he can reveal the hidden wisdom of God to men [*v* 7]. Thus the passage proves the personality and divinity of the Spirit by ascribing intelligent activity and omniscience to him.

*V*11: **For who among men knoweth the things of a man, save the spirit of the man, which is in him? even so the things of God none knoweth, save the Spirit of God.**

As no one can know the things of a man except the spirit of the man that is 'in him', so no one can understand the things of God apart from the Spirit of God. The omission of 'in him' from the second part of the verse shows that Paul's analogy must not be pressed beyond its immediate purpose: 'for in the case of ourselves, we and our own spirit are *numerically one;* whereas in this very passage – and in every other place where the Holy Spirit is spoken of – there is observed *a distinction of conscious personality* between "God" on the one hand and the "Spirit of God" on the other' (David Brown).

V12: **But we received, not the spirit of the world, but the spirit which is from God; that we might know the things that were freely given to us of God.**

But *we* received, not that spirit of human wisdom which permeates a fallen world, but rather the Spirit which is of God. For 'to whatever degree of power this spirit of the world may rise, it cannot give man the knowledge of the divine plans, nor make an apostle even of the greatest genius' (Godet). The aorist tenses of the verbs show that until the Spirit is imparted in regeneration there can be no personal participation in the blessings of the gospel. Hence Findlay remarks that the historic gifts of God to men in Christ 'would have been idle boons without the Spirit enabling us to "know" them' [cf *Eph* 1:17ff].

V13: **Which things also we speak, not in words which man's wisdom teacheth, but which the Spirit teacheth; combining spiritual things with spiritual *words*.**

Paul here refers to himself and the nature of his ministry in Corinth: 'which things we speak out, not in words taught by man's wisdom, but in those words which are taught by the Spirit'. The apostle could not proclaim a spiritual message in words of natural wisdom, and this was why he preached as he did. The Corinthians found his speech insipid because it lacked the savour of worldly wisdom, but their complaint merely showed that they still had a carnal palate [3:1; 2 *Cor* 10:10]. For no words but those which are instinct with the divine life of the Spirit have the power to vivify the spiritually dead.

combining spiritual things with spiritual *words.* In short, not only has the Spirit revealed these things to Paul, but he also ensures that they are exactly transmitted to others through the very words which he teaches. 'Both the spiritual things and the spiritual words that convey them emanate equally from the Spirit, and the apostles combine the two accordingly. This is Paul's definition of Verbal Inspiration' (Lenski).

*V*14: **Now the natural man receiveth not the things of the Spirit of God: for they are foolishness unto him; and he cannot know them, because they are spiritually judged.**

Now the natural man This man may be of the noblest character and attainments in the estimation of the world, yet he lacks the one thing needful. He is described as the natural man because his nature is unchanged by grace. As a stranger to the new birth [*John* 3:3–8], he is 'one who lives on the purely material plane, without being touched by the Spirit of God' (Arndt-Gingrich). Hence he not only lacks the capacity to receive the things of the Spirit, but he also rejects them as foolishness [cf *Rom* 8:7].

because they are spiritually examined. (ASV margin) The fact that Paul uses this word *anakrinō* no less than ten times in this Epistle, though in no other, may suggest that it was a catchword among his critics in Corinth (Barrett). It is a legal term which refers to 'the preliminary examination, preceding the trial proper' (A. Souter). Although the unconverted presume to pass judgment on the gospel after giving it a first hearing, the absurdity of this procedure is at once revealed by their total incapacity to sift its content. 'The unspiritual are out of court as religious critics; they are deaf men judging music' (Findlay).

*V*15: **But he that is spiritual judgeth all things, and he himself is judged of no man.**

But he that is spiritual examineth all things, (ASV margin) It is because the spiritual man is a man whose mind has been illuminated by the Holy Spirit that he has the discernment to evaluate 'all things' in the light of that revelation; whereas the natural man is not only blind to the glory of the gospel, but is also without the ability to reach a right judgment on even the common things of this life because he lacks the perception which would enable him to see their true meaning and purpose (Lenski).

and he himself is examined of no man. (ASV margin) As most of this letter is taken up with the sifting of spiritual men, 'no man' must here refer to the natural man. Paul's meaning is that the man who is without the Spirit has no means of judging the spiritual man. 'Since none other possesses the probe of truth furnished by the Spirit of God; the spiritual man stands on a height from which he overlooks the world, and is overlooked only by God. The statement is ideal, holding good of "the spiritual man" as, and so far as, he is such. Where a Christian is carnal [3:1], his spiritual judgment is vitiated; to that extent he puts himself within the measure of the natural man' (Findlay).

*V*16: **For who hath known the mind of the Lord, that he should instruct him? But we have the mind of Christ.**

Paul makes the prophet's question his own [*Is* 40:13]. The

Corinthians with all their vaunted wisdom feel free to find fault with the preaching of an inspired apostle. Then perhaps they should go on to instruct the King from whom the ambassador received his message! 'To the Corinthians, Paul brought the mind of Christ and made them share in the divine gospel wisdom. Will they now fall back into their former state and with worldly wisdom tell the Lord how to improve his mind and to make the gospel wisdom what they think it ought to be?' (Lenski). All those who still rely on their own ideas to 'improve' the gospel cannot escape this grave indictment of blasphemy.

But we have the mind of Christ. Since none but Christ knows the mind of God, it is only through the revelation given to him by Christ that Paul is made to share in this knowledge of the divine purpose. 'Thus the minister of a sovereign could say, after an intimate conversation with his king, I am in full possession of my master's mind. From this moment, therefore, to criticize the servant is to criticize the master' (Godet). The apostles had committed to them a revelation of supreme authority so that afterwards it might spread 'by degrees to the whole church' (Calvin). It is therefore by their response to this declaration of the Lord's once hidden plan of salvation that believers are said to possess 'the mind of Christ', which clearly may not be equated with a state of mindless mysticism [cf 1 *Pet* 1:13].

CHAPTER THREE

At first Paul's plain preaching of the gospel was due to the fact that the Corinthians were mere babes in Christ, but it is a matter of reproof that he is still unable to feed them with meat. For they had shown how spiritually immature they were by making their favourite preachers the subject of party strife in the church [vv 1–4]. Instead of glorying in men they should understand that ministers are not rivals competing for their loyalty, but fellow-servants engaged in the common task of building God's church. Paul has laid the one true foundation, and now others must take care how they build upon it. The jerry-builder will suffer the disgrace of seeing his work destroyed, but the faithful workman will be rewarded for his labours [vv 5–15]. As the Corinthians are God's temple, they must realize that if any man defiles God's dwelling-place, God will destroy him [vv 16, 17]. Hence they are to renounce that worldly wisdom which foolishly glories in men. For all things, including their ministers, belong to them, even as they belong to Christ [vv 18–23].

V1: **And I, brethren, could not speak unto you as unto spiritual, but as unto carnal, as unto babes in Christ.**

And I, brethren, 'He reproveth, yet keeps up his love . . . Some have observed in the Old Testament, the *Prophets* in their Sermons were more severe, *Thus saith the Lord*, and they never called their Auditors *Brethren*; but in the *Gospel*, a dispensation of love, there is often *Brethren, and I beseech you by the mercies of Christ*' (Anthony Burgess).

could not speak unto you as unto spiritual, but as unto carnal, Paul reminds his readers that the content of his teaching during the early days of his mission in Corinth was determined by their condition at that time. He could not then address them as spiritual men [2:15], but only as those who were still 'fleshy' in their modes of thought and action. 'The *I could not* is an implicit answer to the disdainful charge of his enemies. "He knew not"' (Godet).

as unto babes in Christ. Immaturity during infancy is normal, but if that condition is unduly prolonged the result is monstrous. The Corinthians had undergone a radical change, a new principle of life had been implanted within them. They were now 'in Christ', but it was not intended that they should remain '*babes* in Christ' for ever [13:11, 14:20]. Life must develop and they are to press on to perfection. It is tragic that so many believers remain in the spiritual kindergarten long after they ought to have been teachers of the gospel [Heb 5:12]. 'Paul's goal was for all babes to become adults [Col 1:28]' (A. T. Robertson).

*V*2: **I fed you with milk, not with meat; for ye were not yet able *to bear it:* nay, not even now are ye able;**

It would be quite wrong to infer from this that Paul preached the elementary doctrines to beginners and reserved the advanced teaching for the mature, for he always preached 'the whole counsel of God' [Acts 20:27]. The distinction is not between two sets of doctrines but between two ways of presenting the same gospel. 'For the same Christ is milk for babes, and solid food for adults' (Calvin). So our Lord himself condescended to teach the Word to the people in many parables as they 'were able to hear it' [*Mark* 4:33]. But with the words 'nay, not even now are ye able', Paul shatters the spiritual complacency of the Corinthians by an abrupt return to the present tense. 'At one time they were naturally immature without special blame; now their immaturity is a different matter . . . "Now" is cumulative: this inability persists contrary to nature and to expectation' (Lenski).

*V*3: **for ye are yet carnal: for whereas there is among you jealousy and strife, are ye not carnal, and do ye not walk after the manner of men?**

for ye are yet carnal: When the Corinthians were but babes in the faith Paul said that they were 'fleshy' (*sarkinos*, *v* 1); here he accuses them of 'fleshly' behaviour, of walking according to the flesh (*sarkikos*). Although many authorities are doubtful whether there is any difference in meaning between these words, A. T. Robertson says that 'a real distinction seems to be observed' in 1 *Cor* 3:1 and 3:3 (*A Grammar of the Greek New Testament*, p. 158). Paul is blaming them for their unspiritual conduct, for though they have received the Spirit, they are still acting as 'men' [*v* 4], i.e. as those who belong to the flesh and are characterized by it.

for whereas there is among you jealousy and strife, 'The proof is from the effects. For since jealousy, disputes and factions are fruits of the flesh, we can be sure that, wherever they are to be seen, there flourishes the root. These evils held sway among the Corinthians; therefore from that Paul shows clearly that they were carnal' (Calvin) [*Gal* 5:15-26].

are ye not carnal, and do ye not walk after the manner of men? 'Oh what *Antipodes* are such men to the Scripture! Either lay down the name of a Christian, or else live above what men of the world do. As *Alexander* said to a soldier named *Alexander*. Either lay aside his name, or else do valiant acts' (Burgess).

V4: **For when one saith, I am of Paul; and another, I am of Apollos; are ye not men?**

'Although they did not advance the names and persons of wicked men, but of holy and eminent men, yet by these names of holy men, they made unholy and wicked divisions. Observe, *That when the Devil cannot hurt the Church by a profane and sinful Ministry, then he labours to destroy it by abusing the names and esteem of those who are truly holy and eminent* . . . so the Devil when he cannot destroy souls by stirring up wicked instruments, he will endeavour that men should think of good instruments more than they ought' (Burgess) [cf 1:12].

V5: **What then is Apollos? and what is Paul? Ministers through whom ye believed; and each as the Lord gave to him.**

These rhetorical questions drive home the folly of making 'ministers' the leaders of parties. Apollos and Paul are merely 'servants' (*diakonoi*: a word which underlines the lowly character of their service), while the preposition 'through' (*dia*) also marks the purely instrumental character of this service. Moreover, as befits subordinates, 'each' servant was assigned his particular task, 'as the Lord gave to him'; and each performed his own duty (Barrett).

V6: **I planted, Apollos watered; but God gave the increase.**

'The Metaphor is easy. As the Gardener sets his herbs, waters them, but he cannot make them grow, he cannot make the least flower that is, though he hath never so much skill: Thus it is here, though they be Ministers of *Seraphical* affections, and *Cherubinical* knowledge, yet they cannot make the Word to prosper, and to increase in the hearer; it is God who doth that, *Isaiah* 55:10; 61:11. There you have such similitudes; so that this . . . is an admirable direction to look above the abilities, above the parts and gifts of men: We think, Oh if we have such a Ministry, all would be well! whereas *Apollos* and *Paul* cannot give the increase' (Burgess).

*V*7: **So then neither is he that planteth anything, neither he that watereth; but God that giveth the increase.**

The emphasis falls on the final word in the Greek sentence, which is 'God'. It is *God* that gives the increase. 'Men are but God's instruments, tools, "agents" (ministers) in performing this work. They do not act in it for God, that is, instead of God; but God acts through them . . . This is Paul's teaching everywhere: that as it is God who created us men, so it is God who has recreated us Christians. And the one in as direct and true a sense as the other. As He used agents in the one case – our natural generation (for none of us are born men without parents) – so He may use instruments in the other, our spiritual regeneration (for none of us are born Christians where there is no Word). But in both cases, it is God and God alone who gives the increase' (B. B. Warfield, 'Man's Husbandry and God's Bounty', *Faith and Life*, pp. 211–221).

*V*8: **Now he that planteth and he that watereth are one: but each shall receive his own reward according to his own labour.**

All who engage in this spiritual husbandry are in the same honourable employment. So if one plants and another waters, it is all 'one', because both are fellow-labourers under God, who will reward each 'according to his own labour'. 'Wages are measured by labour, not results. And therefore it is all one to you and me, as labourers in God's field, whether He sets us to plough, plant, water or reap . . . The amount of labour, not the department of work, is the norm of our reward. What a consolation this is to the obscure workman to whom God has given much labour and few results; reward is proportioned to the labour, not the results!' (Warfield, *op. cit.*).

*V*9: **For we are God's fellow-workers: ye are God's husbandry, God's building.**

We are fellow-labourers in the service of God: (Arndt-Gingrich) This alternative rendering of the Greek is to be preferred as being more consistent with context, which stresses the fact that Paul and Apollos are not rivals but joint-workers in God's service. Thus the first part of the verse refers to God's ministers, and the second to God's people. But though both belong to God, he has entrusted his ministers with the task of calling his people to faith in Christ and bringing them to spiritual maturity. 'The Corinthians acted as if these ministers were theirs, to be measured and weighed at pleasure, to be exalted or to be lowered, to be rewarded with praise or to be chastised with criticism. Paul takes these ministers out of their hands, they are God's, doing his work under his special call and commission' (Lenski).

ye are God's husbandry, God's building. Their work is not completed, but is still in progress. The field is under cultivation; the building is in course of construction. 'The former of these metaphors has been already applied [*vv* 6–8]: and now the latter is expanded [*vv* 10–17]. Thus "God's husbandry, God's building" is the link which connects the two paragraphs together. Of the two images "husbandry" implies the organic growth of the church, "building" the mutual adaptation of its parts' (Lightfoot).

*V*10: **According to the grace of God which was given unto me, as a wise masterbuilder I laid a foundation; and another buildeth thereon. But let each man take heed how he buildeth thereon.**

Although Paul freely ascribes all the praise to the grace of God, his fickle readers needed to be reminded that the church in Corinth owed its very existence to his labours there. It was he and none other who had laid a foundation as a skilful masterbuilder. It now remains the solemn responsibility of each one who continues the work to see that he builds worthily on that foundation. The apostle 'uses three metaphors to express the respective relations of himself and of other teachers to the Corinthian church. He is planter [6], founder [10], and father [4:15]. Apollos and the rest are waterers, after-builders, and tutors' (Robertson – Plummer).

*V*11: **For other foundation can no man lay than that which is laid, which is Jesus Christ.**

Paul is confident that his work will endure because the foundation he laid corresponds with that which is already laid by God. 'The foundation laid by Paul [*v* 10] was Christ preached and taught in the work of his crucifixion, and afterwards of his resurrection. The foundation already laid by God [*v* 11] was Christ Jesus himself, crucified and risen. The same cornerstone in different fashion was laid by both. *Essentially* by the divine Architect in heaven, *Doctrinally* by his inspired masterbuilder on earth' (T. C. Hammond). This means that Christianity is the historical realization of the eternal purpose of God. It is this fact which manifests the folly of those religious teachers who expect to build an eternal edifice on some other purely temporal foundation. For it is certain that the beliefs which originate in this world are by their very nature quite unable to transcend it. In thus distinguishing himself from the foundation [cf 2 *Cor* 4:5],

Paul may have been implicitly condemning those in Corinth who did not hesitate to identify another apostle with it. If so, it seems reasonable to suppose that some in the Peter-party were claiming that *their* leader was the true foundation of the church, even though Peter's own testimony was very different [cf *Matt* 16:16, 18; 1 *Pet* 2:6].

*V*12: **But if any man buildeth on the foundation gold, silver, costly stones, wood, hay, stubble;**

But whereas some will build upon the true foundation with precious materials, others may think fit to use base materials which will not withstand the testing fire of God's judgment. The first group presents the pure doctrine which is in keeping with the foundation, while the second stands for that teaching which is unworthy of it. 'He doth not by hay and stubble speak of such dangerous and damnable heresies that overthrow the foundation, such are not saved, though by fire, but they bring upon themselves swift damnation [2 *Peter* 2:1] but lesser errors and falsehoods, which do not overthrow, yet are no ways agreeable or suitable to the foundation' (Burgess).

*V*13: **each man's work shall be made manifest: for the day shall declare it, because it is revealed in fire; and the fire itself shall prove each man's work of what sort it is.**

On the Day of Judgment the work of every preacher shall be subjected to the searching scrutiny of the Lord which is here likened to a consuming fire [2 *Cor* 5:10, 11]. The key to Paul's imagery is to be found in the prophecy of Malachi which depicts the Lord's sudden coming to his temple in fiery judgment [*Mal* 3:1, 2; cf 2 *Thess* 1:8].

each man's work 'The unity of structure makes it impossible for men to distinguish the work of one builder from that of another. God only can say where the work of one man ends and that of another begins. The extent no less than the quality of the work will be judged' (Edwards).

and the fire itself shall prove each man's work of what sort it is. The work is *proved* in the expectation that something good will be found in it. 'But it must be kept in mind that Paul does not imply that something good will be found in every instance, a thought definitely excluded by the reference to wood, hay and stubble which will be burnt completely' (Grosheide).

*V*14: **If any man's work shall abide which he built thereon, he shall receive a reward.**

He whose work survives this stringent test shall receive a wage for work well done. 'This reward cannot be salvation; for the faithful workman was already in possession of this supreme blessing when he was labouring. We have to think then of more particular privileges, such as the joy of being the object of the Master's satisfaction: "Good and faithful servant!"; then the happiness of seeing invested with glory the souls whom a faithful ministry has contributed to sanctify; finally, the possession of a glorious position in the new state of things established by the Lord at his coming: "Thou hast gained ten pounds; receive power over ten cities" [*Luke* 19:17]' (Godet).

*V*15: **If any man's work shall be burned, he shall suffer loss: but he himself shall be saved; yet so as through fire.**

On the other hand, the man who tries to build with wood, hay or stubble will see all his work destroyed in the fire of divine judgment, and lose the reward he expects to receive. This 'burning up denotes the complete rejection of the work of the unwise builders, their teaching and all that they thought they had accomplished in men's hearts through it' (Lenski). So because it is better to be sure now than sorry later, each preacher should take pains to find out whether he is exercising a fireproof ministry.

but he himself shall be saved; 'The man himself will be saved, though his work will be burned. As a worker he suffers loss; but his salvation is through faith. Yet his salvation even will be through the fire of conflagration that consumes his work. He deserves for his unfaithfulness to forfeit his salvation and perish with the unbeliever. But he is saved as if through the very flames. He is a smoking firebrand' (Edwards). [*Zech* 3:2; *Jude* 23].

yet so as through fire. As Godet so clearly shows, no support for the Romish fiction of purgatory can be claimed from this passage. 'This is to forget, – 1. that the fire is allegorical like the building; 2. that it is only teachers who are in question; 3. that the trial indicated is a means of valuation, not of purification; 4. that this fire is lighted at Christ's coming, and consequently does not yet burn in the interval between the death of Christians and that advent; 5. that the salvation of the worker, of which Paul speaks, takes place not *by*, but *in spite of* the fire'.

*V*16: **Know ye not that ye are a temple of God, and** *that* **the Spirit of God dwelleth in you?**

The character of this building is now described: the Corinthians are nothing less than God's temple ('the omission of the article merely concentrates attention on the character of the society, and does not describe them as one of many shrines' – St. John Parry). But as is so often the case in this Epistle, the information is conveyed in the form of a question which is fraught with rebuke, 'Know ye not?' [cf 5:6, 6:2, 6:3, 6:9, 6:15, 6:16, 6:19, 9:13, 9:24]. It is indeed a serious matter to build badly upon the true foundation, but to defile the very dwelling-place of God is far worse [*v* 17]. Paul's stern warning is evidently addressed to those who are disturbing the unity of the church by their party strife [cf 1:13: 'Is Christ divided?']. For in virtue of the indwelling presence of the Holy Spirit they all together constitute the true temple of God, whose peace cannot be shattered without sacrilege.

*V*17: **If any man destroyeth the temple of God, him shall God destroy; for the temple of God is holy, and such are ye.**

If any man destroyeth the temple of God, him shall God destroy; That the punishment fits the crime is indicated by the repetition of the verb, for the desecration of the divine sanctuary is a capital offence. Thus he who destroys God's temple will be destroyed by God, i.e. punished 'with eternal destruction' (Arndt-Gingrich).

for the temple of God is holy, As the earthly temple was set apart for holy use and could not be profaned with impunity, so Christians are consecrated to God and cannot be 'defiled by any as instruments in that action, without exceeding great peril and hazard to them that endeavour and attempt any such thing' (Poole).

and such are ye. '*The holy Temple of God under the Gospel, is not any place, though never so adorned or glorious; but persons believing and worshipping of Him according to His will.* This Doctrine hath its great use. For once in God's Church, while Popery and her principles reigned, all the holiness spoken of, preached for, pleaded for principally, was holiness of things, not persons; holy Temples, holy Altars, holy Images; but real, personal holiness, which God commands, was despised and opposed . . . The Temple, the Church of God, are

Persons believing. The Image of God is righteousness and holiness in our lives' (Burgess).

*V*18: **Let no man deceive himself. If any man thinketh that he is wise among you in this world, let him become a fool, that he may become wise.**

In conclusion Paul urges the Corinthians to renounce the worldly wisdom which had divided rather than edified the church [*vv* 18–23]. Each man is warned that his cherished preconceptions are no more than self-deceptions. '*Human conceited wisdom must needs hinder the entertainment of Christ's truth, because it sets itself on the Throne to be Judge, and to determine truth or falsehood according to her own principles. It makes weights and a standard of its own, and will weigh even what God and the Scripture saith, by its own self*' (Burgess). In other words, all *autonomous* thought is *apostate* thought, because the thinking that begins with man can never end with God. Dependent creatures, who have received the candle of reason from God, must be humble enough to think God's thoughts after him.

If any man thinketh that he is wise among you in this world, 'Men must not think to be wise in both spheres; the church's wise are the world's fools, and *vice versa*. The cross is "foolishness" to the world, and he who espouses it a "fool" in its opinion – a *fool* with a *criminal* for his Master; and one can only be a Christian sage – wise after the manner of ch 2:8ff – upon condition of bearing this reproach. Paul was crazy in the eyes of the world [4:10; 2 *Cor* 5:13; *Acts* 26:24], but how wise *amongst us*!' (Findlay).

let him become a fool, that he may become wise. This 'is only in *appearance*, and in the judgment of the world; he speaketh by concession; the world will judge all true Scripture and heavenly wisdom to be foolishness. So that as the world's wisdom is a real folly, but a seeming wisdom: so the Scripture-wisdom, is a real wisdom, but a seeming folly' (Burgess).

*V*19: **For the wisdom of this world is foolishness with God. For it is written, He that taketh the wise in their craftiness:**

It is because God's judgment of the wisdom of this world is not determined by 'the outward appearance', but is based on his perfect knowledge of all things in their inner reality, that it must be accepted as true [1 *Sam* 16:7]. 'There are many wise, learned men in the world, whose naked propositions we do more regard than other men's demonstrations. But how much more should we acquiesce in God's assertions? We may justly call all human wisdom mere foolishness, because God doth so' (Burgess). Since the Corinthians found this truth so hard to accept, Paul not only repeats it [cf 1:20], but also invokes the testimony of Scripture to confirm it [*Job* 5:13]. The words are taken from the speech of Eliphaz who was also a wise man of this world. The apostle uses the statement which is true in itself without in any way endorsing the wrong application that Eliphaz makes of it. Similarly, in addressing the philosophers of Athens Paul felt free to quote the words of heathen poets for he recognized that 'pagan men, in spite of themselves and contrary to the controlling disposition of their minds, as creatures of God confronted with the divine revelation were capable of responses which were valid so long as and to the extent that they stood in isolation from their pagan systems' (Stonehouse) [*Acts* 17:28].

*V*20: **and again, The Lord knoweth the reasonings of the wise, that they are vain.**

Psalm 94:11 is the second testimony which Paul brings forward to prove his case. Under the inspiration of the Spirit he applies what was originally spoken of 'man' to a particular class of men, for what is true of the vanity of human thought in general is especially relevant to 'the reasonings of the wise'. Such men entertain high hopes for their schemes, but God knows beforehand that these will be void of the expected result. Thus their thoughts are futile because they always leave God out of their reckoning [cf *Rom* 1:21].

*V*21a: **Wherefore let no one glory in men.**

Paul now states the only proper conclusion to be drawn from the preceding argument. This verse is the counterpart of 1:31 It is because the Corinthians are bidden to 'glory in the Lord' that they are forbidden to 'glory in men'. Yet this was precisely what they were doing, for the God-ordained relationship with their teachers was reversed by their partisan applause. For when they said, I belong to Paul or Apollos or Peter, they forgot that by the grace of God these men belonged to them [cf 2 *Cor* 4:5].

*V*21b: **For all things are yours;**
*V*22: **whether Paul, or Apollos, or Cephas, or the world, or life, or death, or things present, or things to come; all are yours;**
*V*23: **and ye are Christ's; and Christ is God's.**

Having finished his exhortation, Paul is able to end with a passage of great lyrical beauty in which he sets forth the manifold privileges of the people of God in a way that recalls *Rom* 8:31–39.

For all things are yours; 'The Christian loses this birthright by treating the world or its interests as ends in themselves, i.e. by becoming enslaved to persons [7:23; 2 *Cor* 11:20] or things [6:12; *Phil* 3:19] . . . The Corinthians, by boasting in men, were forgetting, and thereby imperilling, their prerogative in Christ' (Robertson – Plummer).

whether Paul, or Apollos, or Cephas, Because God puts his servants at the disposal of the church, they are *all* the property of the congregation [4:1f]. 'At Corinth they were choosing one of these men and rejecting others. That is foolishness, it is the wisdom of the world, for God gave them all' (Grosheide).

or the world, God preserves the world so 'that He may attain the ends of His Predestination. Insomuch that there had been no Creation at first, no world at all, nor would there still be any sustentation, or conservation of it, were it not for the Church's sake' (Burgess) [*Rom* 8:28–30].

or life, or death, 'This means not merely that the question whether the people of God live or die, is determined with reference to their own good; but also that life and death are dispensed and administered so as best to fulfil the designs of God in reference to the church. The greatest men of the world, kings, statesmen and heroes, ministers, individual believers and unbelievers, live or die just as best subserves the interests of Christ's kingdom' (Hodge).

or things present, or things to come; The first phrase includes all that can happen to us in this present life; while the second points to the forthcoming transformation, with its eternal consequences.

all are yours; Paul repeats his assertion that 'all things' belong to believers, not only to sum up the preceding enumeration, but also to stress the contrast between this sweeping statement and the phrase with which he immediately qualifies it.

and ye are Christ's; 'The Corinthian readers, exalted to a height outsoaring Stoic pride, are in a moment laid low at the feet of Christ: "Lords of the universe – you are his bondmen, your vast heritage in the present and future you gather as *factors for him*" . . . Our property is immense, but *we* are Another's; we rule, to be ruled. A man cannot own too much, provided that *he recognizes his Owner*' (Findlay).

and Christ is God's. The official title 'Christ' makes it plain that the reference is to the Son's voluntary or 'economic' subjection to the Father as Mediator. As the Messiah, 1. He received a people from God in the eternal covenant of redemption [*John* 17:2]; 2. He became obedient in life and death to the will of the Father [*Phil* 2:7, 8]; 3. He is exalted by God to exercise universal lordship as the Head of the redeemed community 'till he hath put all enemies under his feet' [15:24; *Acts* 5:31; *Phil* 2:9, 10].

'Is Christ thus wholly God's? Then what self-denial, what humility and modesty should we learn hence? Shall Christ not seek His own glory? Shall not He seek to please Himself? Shall not He exalt His own will? Why then are we so apt to magnify our self-glory, our own will, our own advantage? It should shame us who follow such a Christ, to be called by the name of this Christ; How ill do such an Head, and such members agree together? Think of Christ, when pride, vain-glory, self-will, stirreth in thee: *If Christ had been thus, there had been no pardon, no salvation for me*' (Burgess).

CHAPTER FOUR

All this means that the Corinthians should regard their ministers as the servants of Christ and stewards of the mysteries of God. Hence Paul is not concerned with how men may estimate the value of his ministry when the only competent judge of his labours is the Lord to whom he is accountable [vv 1–5]. They have no right to prefer one teacher above another when these men have all received their differing gifts from God [vv 6–7]. Paul ironically contrasts the vain spirit that leads them to make such arrogant judgments with his own despised and afflicted state [vv 8–13]. As their one father in Christ, he writes these things not to shame them, but to urge them to follow him [vv 14, 15]. He had sent Timothy to remind them of his teaching, but hopes soon to come in person when his critics shall have full proof of his authority. The character of his visit will be determined by their response to his reproofs: Is he to come with a rod, or in a spirit of meekness? [vv 17–21].

V1: **Let a man so account of us, as of ministers of Christ, and stewards of the mysteries of God.**

A wrong estimate of the servants of Christ has been the occasion of strife in Corinth. Now the apostle proceeds to indicate their true place in the church. The Corinthians are to consider them first of all, not as heads of parties, or even as ministers of the church, but as 'Christ's underlings' (NEB);

men without any authority of their own, whose sole business is to execute the commands of their Lord. The word, which originally referred to 'under-rowers', here points to the lowliness of their service. Secondly, they must be recognized as 'God's stewards'; a term showing that they have been dignified with the responsible task of declaring God's 'mysteries' to all men. Accordingly their commission is not to disseminate their own ideas, but to preach a divinely revealed gospel [cf 2:7].

V2: **Here, moreover, it is required in stewards, that a man be found faithful.**

And in the realm of stewardship, trustworthiness is the principal thing. In the eyes of his master, nothing can compensate for the lack of fidelity in a steward, whatever other good qualities he may be seen to possess [*Luke* 16:1ff]. The Corinthians presumed to judge ministers by their *gifts*, whereas *faithfulness* is the primary and indispensable requirement. And who but God himself is competent to judge that? 'Responsible not to his fellows, but *to the Lord*, his high trust demands a strict account [*Luke* 12:41–48]' (Findlay).

V3: **But with me it is a very small thing that I should be judged of you, or of man's judgment: yea, I judge not mine own self.**

Since the faithful steward always has in view the final reckoning with his master, whether he stands or falls in the estimation of his fellow-servants is of little moment to him [*Rom* 14:4; I *Pet* 4:10]. Thus as far as he is concerned, Paul regards it as of the smallest consequence that the Corinthians should take it upon themselves to examine his character, motives, and methods. This does not mean that he was not hurt by their criticism, but that he was not moved by it. As he did not receive his message from men, neither their praise nor their blame is to deflect the steward of God's mysteries from his solemn obligation faithfully to fulfil his ministry [*Acts* 20:26, 27; 2 *Tim* 4:2]. Paul's curious reference to 'man's day' (ASV margin) contrasts the judgment of men with the Lord's judgment-day [3:13]. '*That* is the tribunal which the apostle recognizes; a *human* tribunal he does not care to satisfy' (Robertson-Plummer).

*V*4: **For I know nothing against myself; yet am I not hereby justified: but he that judgeth me is the Lord.**

As Calvin points out, Paul is not protesting sinlessness, but claiming that he has carried out his duties as an apostle 'with so much integrity and faithfulness that his conscience did not accuse him in any way'. Nevertheless he refuses to anticipate Christ's judgment on his labours. For though conscience can 'judge' and control conduct in the world, this subjective faculty is powerless to pronounce the final verdict on a man's life. Consequently the word 'justified' here has nothing to do with the sinner's justification by faith [*Rom* 3:24]; it refers to the judicial acquittal of God's steward when the divine sentence of approval is passed upon his work on the last day [cf 3:14]. In referring the judgment of his ministry to the Lord, Paul does not mean 'that all ministers are to be given a free hand to do what they think is right until the Lord at last judges them. What Paul says is that men must not usurp the Lord's judgment-seat and judge the Lord's ministers according to their own wisdom. Paul does not for one moment judge himself in this way. Yet the Corinthians were judging their ministers in this manner. Men do it to this day' (Lenski).

*V*5: **Wherefore judge nothing before the time, until the Lord come, who will both bring to light the hidden things of darkness, and make manifest the counsels of**

the hearts; and then shall each man have his praise from God.

The Corinthians must stop passing such premature judgments on the Lord's servants, for only he can judge them, and this he will do at his coming. Yet they were not only guilty of judging what was beyond their jurisdiction, but also of failing to judge that which did fall within its scope [cf 5:12; 6:1–5]. How foolish they were in pretending to see what they had no means of discerning when they remained blind to what lay before their very eyes!

The brightness of Christ's advent will reveal the true character of those things which were previously hidden by darkness. These are not necessarily *evil* things, but things 'impenetrable to present light' (Findlay). This infallible verdict will be secured by Christ's perfect knowledge of the hearts of all men, for he alone is able to judge the secret motives which determine the quality of each man's work, whether it be good or evil [2 *Cor* 5:10].

and then shall each man have his praise from God. 'Then' *every* faithful steward shall receive his *due* praise, and not just the favourite party-leaders! 'The world praises its princes, generals, ambassadors, wise men, artists: God will hereafter praise his ministers' (Bengel).

*V*6: **Now these things, brethren, I have in a figure transferred to myself and Apollos for your sakes; that in us ye might learn not *to go* beyond the things which are written; that no one of you be puffed up for the one against the other.**

I have applied all this to myself and Apollos (RSV) i.e. 'I have given this teaching of mine the form of an exposition concerning Apollos and myself' (Arndt-Gingrich). In 3:4–6 Paul expressed himself in terms which showed that no criticism of Apollos was intended, but if Judaizing teachers had arrived in Corinth and were invoking Peter's authority as a cloak for their activities, he could not mention Peter's name without seeming to blame him for their errors [cf comment on 3:11].

I have done this for your sakes, so that by our example you may learn the lesson, "Not above what is written;" (F. F. Bruce). By freely ascribing all the glory to God for the work which he had accomplished through them, Paul and Apollos had not gone beyond the testimony of Scripture [cf Paul's citation of *Jer* 9:23, 24 in 1:31]. Accordingly their example did not provide the Corinthians with any excuse for elevating them as the heads of rival cliques within the church. But there were other teachers in Corinth who did not scruple to arrogate to themselves the honour that belonged to God alone.

that no one of you be puffed up for the one against the other. 'To cry up a favourite leader of your own choosing is to betray an inflated self-conceit' (Robertson – Plummer).

*V*7: **For who maketh thee to differ? and what hast thou that thou didst not receive? but if thou didst receive it, why dost thou glory as if thou hadst not received it?**
Who has distinguished you? (i.e. as compared with others: cf F. Büchsel, *TDNT*, Vol.III, p.946). A sharp shaft to puncture the Corinthians' presumptuous conceit, for pardoned sinners can boast of nothing but the *distinguishing* grace of God!

and what hast thou that thou didst not receive? Paul's second 'home-thrust' charges them with ingratitude. Those who owe everything to their generous Benefactor clearly have nothing of *their own* in which they can boast. It is worth recalling that this question had a decisive influence on Augustine. He says that he laboured hard to answer it in terms of human ability, but the grace of God won the day. It was through the challenge of Pelagius and the study of Paul's writings, and especially of this verse and of *Rom* 9:16, that there 'had crystallized in his mind the distinctively Augustinian doctrines of man's total depravity, of irresistible grace, and of absolute predestination' (Robertson – Plummer).

but if thou didst receive it, why dost thou glory as if thou hadst not received it? The only possible conclusion which can be drawn from the replies demanded by the first two questions is expressed with unassailable logic in this final thrust. Paul intends it to reduce the articulate Corinthians to speechless shame.

*V*8: **Already are ye filled, already ye are become rich, ye have come to reign without us: yea and I would that ye did reign, that we also might reign with you.**

The Corinthians were behaving as though they had already attained the glories of the coming kingdom, and the emotion which suddenly grips Paul as he contemplates their proud pretensions leads him into a 'long sarcasm' which does not end till *v* 13 'where it is extinguished in grief' (Godet).

Already are ye filled, The apostle has been overtaken by his converts, who have reached the goal before him! They need no longer hunger after righteousness, because they have already taken their seats at the Messianic banquet. They are so puffed up with their favourite teachers and their own fancied attainments in knowledge that they feel like those who have feasted to the full.

already ye are become rich, The thanksgiving [1:5] and the list of gifts in ch 12 'appear to justify this consciousness of wealth; but ostentation corrupted Corinthian riches; spiritual satiety is a sign of arrested growth: contrast *Phil* 3:10-14, and compare *Rev* 3:17, "Thou *sayest*, Rich am I, and I have become rich" ' (Findlay).

without us you have become kings; (RSV) 'While *we* are still exposed to the dangers, sufferings, and shame of the earthly arena [*v* 9], *you* are already reigning in glory with Christ!' 'Thus the rôles have been exchanged: he, the apostle, their "father", must from his lowliness see to what dizzy heights they have attained' (J. Weiss).

yea and I would that ye did reign, that we also might reign with you.
A biting irony which marks an abrupt return to reality. 'Indeed I wish that you did so reign, for then *we* might share *your* triumph!'

*V*9: **For, I think, God hath set forth us the apostles last of all, as men doomed to death: for we are made a spectacle unto the world, both to angels and men.**

For it seems to me that God means us apostles to come in at the very end, like doomed gladiators in the arena! (Moffatt). As the previous verse echoed the catchwords that recall the Stoic maxim, 'I alone am *rich*, I alone *reign* as king'; so here there is probably an allusion to the Stoic idea of the philosopher's conflict with adverse fate which is played out before the gods. G. Kittel says that in this use 'deity is a spectator of the battle which man himself fights in the proud autonomy of his heroism'. But because God is pleased to make the *weakness* of his apostles the vehicle of his *divine power* [cf 2 *Cor* 12:9, 10], those who watch the unequal struggle 'think they see something quite different from that which is really enacted in this *theatre*' (*TDNT*, Vol. III, p.43). For as Christ achieved victory through the seeming defeat

of the cross, so his suffering followers paradoxically triumph
in being 'conquered' by the powers which oppose them – to
the amazement of angels and men! 'The blood of the martyrs
is the seed of the church' (Tertullian). Paul's pathetic description of his own sufferings is a direct challenge to the com-
fortable security of his readers [vv 9-13]. If the heralds of the
gospel are still bearing the cross [Matt 16:24], then how have
their converts managed to precede them to glory?

V10: **We are fools for Christ's sake, but ye are wise in
Christ; we are weak, but ye are strong; ye have glory,
but we have dishonour.**

In this series of striking antitheses, Paul makes his meaning
plain by repeating the words, 'fools, wise, weak, strong'
[1:25ff; 3:18f]: 1. 'It is on Christ's account that we are content
to be labelled the world's *fools*, yet your union with Christ
has made you *wise* in this world!'; 2. 'We confess our personal
weakness, but you are boasting in your own *strength*!'; 3. 'You
have saved your reputation in the world: we have completely
forfeited ours!'

V11: **Even unto this present hour we both hunger,
and thirst, and are naked, and are buffeted, and have no
certain dwelling-place;**
V12a: **and we toil, working with our own hands:**

The imaginary exaltation of the Corinthians is now sharply
contrasted with the actual sufferings which characterize the
life of an apostle 'even unto this present hour'. For fidelity to
his commission involved constant hardship [vv 11, 12a] and
humiliation [vv 12b, 13]. Although Paul speaks in the plural,
it is obvious that his description of these bitter trials is drawn
from his personal experience of them [cf 2 Cor 11:23-29].
He knows what it is to go hungry and thirsty, and 'be poorly
clothed' (Arndt-Gingrich). Often the victim of violent hands,

[71]

always treated as a homeless vagabond, he is also guilty of what the Greeks regarded as the supreme indignity of working with his own hands to support himself [*Acts* 18:3; 2 *Cor* 12:13].

*V*12b: **being reviled, we bless; being persecuted, we endure;**

*V*13: **being defamed, we entreat: we are made as the filth of the world, the offscouring of all things, even until now.**

The present participles denote the habitual treatment meted out to the apostles by their enemies, while the verbs which follow them indicate their habitual response to these cruel acts. They meet insulting abuse with blessings, they hold out under persecution without complaining, and they answer base calumnies with kindly words of entreaty; 'they beseech men not to be so wicked, to return to better feelings, to be converted to Christ' (Godet). In this they followed the teaching and example of their Lord. Yet because meekness was mistaken for weakness, their humility was despised as the mark of an abject, grovelling spirit. Thus in the estimation of the world, the apostles had become the most degraded and despicable of men, the very scum of human society, whose contemptible estate remains unchanged 'even until now'.

*V*14: **I write not these things to shame you, but to admonish you as my beloved children.**

If what Paul had written might well make the Corinthians hang their heads in shame, that was not his purpose in writing; he wrote to 'admonish' them as his 'beloved children'. Because he loved them, he desired their amendment, and his reproofs were directed towards that end. 'His design was to bring the truth to their minds, and let them see what they really were, as contrasted with what they imagined themselves to be' (Hodge).

*V*15: **For though ye have ten thousand tutors in Christ, yet have ye not many fathers; for in Christ Jesus I begat you through the gospel.**

'For if you should have ten thousand tutors in Christ, yet you have not many *fathers*!' However many tutors might follow Paul in Corinth, and whatever respect they were entitled to receive from the Corinthians, it could never exceed that which was owed to their *one* father in the faith [cf 9:2]. 'Paul does not use the title "father" for a Christian minister [cf *Matt* 23:9], but keeps the metaphor for the special purpose of describing the relation between an evangelist and his converts' (Barrett).

for in Christ Jesus I begat you through the gospel. It is only in virtue of Paul's union with Christ and by means of the gospel that he sustains this exceptional relation to them. 'He thus excludes beforehand every appearance of boasting in what he says of himself in the last words: *I begat*. – But if it was Christ who acted with His power and word, it was nevertheless through him, Paul (*egō, I*), that He produced this creation. Hence Paul's right and duty to exhort them, and even admonish them as he does' (Godet).

*V*16: **I beseech you therefore, be ye imitators of me.**

'Then since I am such a father to you, I beseech you to be imitators of me'. Paul has no intention of attracting a partisan following to himself, but rather pleads with the Corinthians to emulate his own example of self-sacrifice in the service of Christ [11:1; 1 *Thess* 1:6; 2 *Thess* 3:7-9]. 'Imitation is the law of the child's life. . . It is one thing to say "I am of Paul" [1:12], another to tread in Paul's steps. The imitation would embrace, in effect, much of what was described in *vv* 9ff.' (Findlay).

*V*17: **For this cause have I sent unto you Timothy, who is my beloved and faithful child in the Lord, who shall put you in remembrance of my ways which are in Christ, even as I teach everywhere in every church.**

'The father sends a son to sons; but a faithful son, which some of them were not' (Edwards) [1 *Tim* 1:2]. It was after Timothy had left Ephesus for Corinth via Macedonia that Paul was advised of the grave situation which had arisen there. Accordingly, he sends this letter by sea, expecting it to arrive before Timothy who was travelling more slowly by land [*Acts* 19:22].

who shall put you in remembrance of my ways which are in Christ, The apostle is confident that the conduct of his faithful son would remind the Corinthians of what had been his own manner of life among them. But it was only because Paul's ways were also those of Christ himself that they became an authoritative pattern for them to follow [*Gal* 2:20]. 'Paul's *ways* and *teaching* are not the same thing; but the former are regulated by the latter; they will find the same consistency in Timothy' (Findlay).

even as I teach everywhere in every church. Once again he reminds his readers that they are no more than a part of a much greater whole. They are neither the whole church, nor the most perfect members of it. But 'no more is required of them than is required of other Christians' (Robertson – Plummer).

*V*18: **Now some are puffed up, as though I were not coming to you.**
*V*19: **But I will come to you shortly, if the Lord will; and I will know, not the word of them that are puffed up, but the power.**

In spite of the confident assertions of his detractors to the contrary, Paul assures the Corinthians that he will indeed visit them shortly, 'if the Lord will', i.e. provided this proposal is in accord with both 'the providential and spiritual government of Christ' (Hodge) [cf 16:7 with *Acts* 16:7]. Then he will prove whether the arrogant boasts of his opponents are matched by their spiritual power. 'Their lack of the Spirit's power to transform men's character was the test by which the apostle intended to try the pretensions of the party-leaders [cf 1 *Thess* 1:5]' (Edwards).

*V*20: **For the kingdom of God is not in word, but in power.**

In their wordy strife the Corinthians appear to have forgotten that the kingdom of God is something more than boastful talk. As in *Rom* 14:17, Paul is not giving an exhaustive definition of the kingdom of God, but is bringing one aspect of it to bear on a particular situation. Since the Corinthians were apparently rejoicing in the blessings of the kingdom without him [*v.* 8], Paul here reminds them that the rule of God in the lives of men cannot be established by mere eloquence. It requires the power of the Spirit to make the preacher's testimony to Christ the means of such a transformation [2:4, 5; 2 *Cor* 5:17].

*V*21: **What will ye? shall I come unto you with a rod, or in love and a spirit of gentleness?**

Paul is resolved to come, but they must decide on the character of their meeting with him. Is it to be a painful or a joyous visit? Shall he come with a rod to administer fatherly chastisement, or in love that expresses itself in a spirit of gentleness? The contrast is between the love that is *concealed* in chastening, and the love that is *revealed* in gentleness. He warns them that if they choose to remain defiant, he will not shrink from using the rod. In that event they would certainly lose

[75]

the sense of his love, but it would not mean that he had ceased to love them [*Heb* 12:7]. This reference to his right to discipline them as an apostle of Jesus Christ concludes the first part of the Epistle, and serves to introduce 'the subject of the following section, which already stirs his wrath' (Findlay).

CHAPTER FIVE

Paul rebukes the Corinthians for tolerating a scandalous case of incest in their midst instead of removing the offender [vv 1, 2]. As they had neglected their duty, Paul has already judged the man as though present with them, in the hope that the faithful exercise of church discipline will lead to his repentance [vv 3-5]. They have no occasion to glory in view of their deplorable failure to maintain the purity of the church by purging out the old leaven of sin [vv 6-8]. Since they had misunderstood a previous letter which forbad them to associate with immoral persons, Paul now explains that the command had reference to church fellowship, and not to necessary social relationships with unbelievers. It was their responsibility to judge the immoral acts of professing Christians, but the sins of outsiders were to be left to the judgment of God [vv 9-13].

*V*1: **It is actually reported that there is fornication among you, and such fornication as is not even among the Gentiles, that one *of you* hath his father's wife.**

Paul expresses the shock of shame which the Corinthians ought to have felt that such a thing should have happened among them. 'Yes, and so heinous a fornication that even the Gentiles utterly condemn what you openly condone!' 'Paul's appeal to this fact is for the purpose of indicating that outside the pale of covenant revelation there was abhorrence of this kind of marital relationship. This implies that the prohibition in question had relevance to mankind in general' (John Murray, *Principles of Conduct*, p. 258).

that one *of you* hath his father's wife. The offence 'may have been marriage of a stepmother after the father's death, but, since the woman is called "his father's wife" (not *widow*), and the act is called *fornication*, it is more likely to be a case of immoral relationship with the father's young second wife' (*The New Bible Dictionary*, p. 789). As Paul does not censure the woman, it must be assumed that she was not a Christian but one of the outsiders whom God would judge [*v* 13]. [*Lev* 18:8, 20:11; *Deut* 22:30; 27:20]

*V*2: **And ye are puffed up, and did not rather mourn, that he that had done this deed might be taken away from among you.**

Paul seeks to awaken a sense of shame in the Corinthians who are still inflated with pride when they ought to have been mourning the loss of a brother slain by sin and dead to God. They did not even grieve over the offence, much less reflect that it was their duty to remove the offender from the church [*v* 13]. 'Their morbid self-importance, which made them so intolerant of petty wrongs [6:7], made them very tolerant of deep disgrace' (Robertson – Plummer).

*V*3: **For I verily, being absent in body but present in spirit, have already as though I were present judged him that hath so wrought this thing,**
*V*4: **in the name of our Lord Jesus, ye being gathered together, and my spirit, with the power of our Lord Jesus,**
*V*5: **to deliver such a one unto Satan for the destruction**

of the flesh, that the spirit may be saved in the day of the Lord Jesus.

But Paul cannot tolerate from a distance what the Corinthians viewed in their midst with complacent indifference, and though absent in body he has already 'judged him that hath *so* wrought *this thing*'. Thus to justify his verdict he has only to point to the shamelessness of the sinner ('so'), and the abominable nature of his sin ('this thing'). The church must give effect to this judgment by meeting together 'in the name of our Lord Jesus', when Paul would be present in spirit to act along with them 'with the power of our Lord Jesus' [cf *Col* 2:5].

to deliver such a one unto Satan for the destruction of the flesh,

Calvin rightly says that this is a fitting way to describe excommunication; 'because, while Christ reigns within, so Satan reigns outside, the church'. But the terms of this sentence surely point to something more than the ordinary exercise of church discipline. According to Henry Alford, This 'was a delegation to the Corinthian church of a *special power, reserved to the Apostles themselves, of inflicting corporeal death or disease* as a punishment for sin'. As notable examples of this extraordinary power, he cites the cases of Ananias and Sapphira [*Acts* 5:1-11], Elymas [*Acts* 13: 8-11], and the blasphemers of 1 *Tim* 1:20. The congregation itself could expel the offender – 'but it could not *deliver to Satan for the destruction of the flesh*, without the authorized concurrence of the Apostle's *spirit, with the power of our Lord Jesus*'.

that the spirit may be saved in the day of the Lord Jesus.

But though Satan is thus permitted to afflict 'the flesh' (i.e. the body as the instrument of sin), the aim of this punishment was the restoration of the sinner, as it would also serve to maintain the purity of the church. In speaking of 'the spirit' being saved in the day of the Lord Jesus, Paul obviously does not envisage a 'disembodied' state of bliss, for he later teaches that the body is to partake of the salvation of the spirit. And this is why he could not speak of the destruction of 'the body', but only of that of 'the flesh' [cf 15:50].

*V*6: **Your glorying is not good. Know ye not that a little leaven leaveneth the whole lump?**

When the Corinthians can so easily tolerate such flagrant immorality it is evident that they have no ground for boasting. In contrast to their fancied attainments, the low spiritual condition of the whole church is proved by the fact that it is found unashamedly glorying despite the presence in their midst of this particular sin!

a little leaven leaveneth the whole lump, cf *Gal* 5:9. 'This proverbial expression is not here intended to express the idea that one corrupt member of the church depraves the whole, because, in the following verses, in which the figure is carried out, the leaven is not *a person*, but *sin*. The idea, therefore, is, that it is the nature of evil to diffuse itself. This is true with regard to individuals and communities' (Hodge).

*V*7: **Purge out the old leaven, that ye may be a new lump, even as ye are unleavened. For our passover also hath been sacrificed,** *even* **Christ:**

As the Jews were obliged to make a thorough search to remove all traces of leaven from their homes before the Passover Feast began, so the Corinthians are completely to remove from their lives every remnant of the sin that belonged to their pagan past. Now they are to be like a freshly mixed lump of dough, to which nothing in the way of yeast has been added. 'The Christian Church is not just the old society patched up. It is radically new' (Leon Morris).

even as ye are unleavened. It is the indicative of grace ('*ye are* unleavened') that provides the indispensable moral dynamic to fulfil the ethical imperative ('*purge out* the old leaven') (Barrett). [cf *Rom* 6:1-11]. Accordingly, they must see to it that their subjective condition corresponds to that objective deliverance from sin which is theirs in Christ.

For our passover also hath been sacrificed, *even* Christ: 'The Jews made sure that all leaven had been removed before they celebrated their Passover, but Christ our Passover has already been sacrificed, and yet the old leaven remains uncleansed from your house!' To say that this is a sacrificial 'metaphor' does not get rid of the meaning which Paul attached to it. He chose to speak of Christ's death in terms of the Passover sacrifice because he saw that there was the same objective necessity for it. In other words, he views the *death* of Christ as the one sacrifice by which the *life* of his people was secured.

*V*8: **wherefore let us keep the feast, not with old leaven, neither with the leaven of malice and wickedness, but with the unleavened bread of sincerity and truth.**

wherefore let us keep festival, (A S V margin) Since our Passover Lamb has been sacrificed, 'let us keep perpetual feast' (Lightfoot). 'The Christian's Paschal feast does not last a week, but all his life' (Godet). This character is given to the Christian's life by the enduring efficacy of Christ's death. As befits those who 'are unleavened' [*v* 7], the Corinthians must feast all their life long on the unleavened bread of sincerity and truth. Sincerity 'is the harmony of our words and actions with our convictions'; truth 'is the harmony of all these with reality' (Edwards). The leaven of the old life which is forbidden to them is defined as consisting of malice and wickedness. There must be no place in their present experience for that evil disposition and those wicked deeds which characterized their former course [cf *Rom* 1:29].

V 9: **I wrote unto you in my epistle to have no company with fornicators;**

'That letter, to which he refers, does not exist today. There is no doubt that many others are lost. But we can rest content that the Lord saw to it that sufficient survive to meet our needs' (Calvin). [cf *John* 21:25 with 20:31]. But some have not scrupled to supply this lack at the expense of the integrity of the letters we do possess. Hence it is confidently affirmed that the lost letter has been 'found' in 2 *Cor* 6:14-7:1, in spite of the fact that there is no manuscript evidence to support this critical flight of fancy! The call in the previous verse for the constant exercise of sincerity and truth may imply that Paul regarded the Corinthians' professed misunderstanding of his previous directive, 'not to mix themselves up together with fornicators', as an excuse for their hesitation to take action against the offender in their midst.

V 10: **not at all *meaning* with the fornicators of this world, or with the covetous and extortioners, or with idolaters; for then must ye needs go out of the world:**

Of course this prohibition did not mean that the Corinthians should avoid all contact with the sinners of this world. Indeed it was impossible to live in a place like Corinth without being in daily touch with those guilty of such vices as fornication, covetousness, and idolatry. But it is one thing to meet them in the market place, and quite another to mix with them in the idol's temple! Paul is not concerned to catalogue every sort of *open sinner*, but mentions 'three classes as being sufficient for

his purpose, namely, that his command concerning fornicators rests on a general principle' (Lenski).

for then must ye needs go out of the world: If the apostle
had intended them to shun all sinners, then they would be
forced to leave the world – a manifestly absurd conclusion.
'The attempt to get "out of the world", in violation of God's
will [*John* 17:15], led to monasticism and its evils' (Fausset).

*V*11: **but as it is, I wrote unto you not to keep company,
if any man that is named a brother be a fornicator, or
covetous, or an idolater, or a reviler, or a drunkard,
or an extortioner; with such a one no, not to eat.**

No, what I meant when I wrote was this: (Bruce) What
should have been obvious to the Corinthians is now made
explicit: Paul summarily forbids them to have fellowship
with any man whose scandalous life belies the name of
'brother'. To the four terms already given he adds two
more: the reviler and the drunkard. Godet expresses the
opinion that the list is 'an unstudied accumulation' from
which order is excluded by disgust. 'With such a one no, not
to eat' refers not to the Lord's supper, but to any kind of
social intercourse [cf 2 *Thess* 3:14]. They are to refuse to
recognize such a man as a 'brother' in the hope that this may
convict him of his sin and lead him to repentance.

*V*12: **For what have I to do with judging them that are
without? Do not ye judge them that are within?**

In the first question Paul harks back to *v* 10, and speaks in the
first person to express the principle that those outside the
communion of the church are beyond its jurisdiction. But in
the second question he reminds the Corinthians that it is their
responsibility to judge all who do claim to be members of the
church [cf *v* 11, 'any man that is named a brother']. While

it is not their province to judge the hearts of their fellow-believers, it is their duty to discipline those who fail to walk worthily of the faith they profess.

*V*13: **But them that are without God judgeth. Put away the wicked man from among yourselves.**

It is not the function of the church to judge outsiders for God judges them. The verb is present because Paul is speaking of disciplinary judging, and not the final judgment [cf 6:2]. But it is the duty of the church 'to expel the offender, and leave him to God's judgment, he having now become one of *them that are without*' (Morris). The apostle's sharp demand for the expulsion of the incestuous person from the congregation is expressed in words taken from *Deut* 17:7, but he changes the verb from the singular to the plural to show that this must be the action of the whole community.

CHAPTER SIX

*Another evil for which Paul rebukes the Corinthians is the scandal
of bringing their disputes before heathen judges, for those who
are destined to judge angels ought to be capable of settling their
differences among themselves. Let them suffer wrong rather than
inflict it upon their fellow-believers [vv 1-8]. Have they forgotten
that evil-doers, such as they once were, shall not enter the kingdom
of God? But now that they have been cleansed from these defile-
ments their behaviour must match their new identity [vv 9-11].
All lawful things are not expedient, and liberty is not licence.
For though food is for the stomach, the body is not for fornication,
but is destined for union with the Lord [vv 12-14]. As believers
are therefore members of Christ and temples of the Holy Spirit,
this sin is a gross profanation of their bodies, which belong to God
and must be used for his glory [vv 15-20].*

*V*1: **Dare any of you, having a matter against his neighbour, go to law before the unrighteous, and not before
the saints?**

The necessity of judging those within the church leads on
naturally to the scandal of submitting disputes between
believers to the judgment of those who do not belong to the
church [vv 1-11]. Paul's shocked question is intended to shame
the Corinthians. 'Dare' is almost an argument in itself: it is by

this grand word that he marks 'the injured majesty of the Christian name' (Bengel). The Jews always settled their differences among themselves since the rabbis held that to take a case before idolatrous judges was blasphemy against the law. But evidently the Greek fondness for litigation had caused the Christians of Corinth to fall below that high standard. They were guilty of this evil because they did not know that it was beneath the dignity of 'the saints' – *those accounted holy through believing* – to call upon 'the unrighteous' – *unjust because unbelieving* – to decide their disputes. Paul is not implying that heathen judges are unjust in their judgments, but is showing that 'to invoke pagan courts to settle lawsuits between believers was a confession of Christian failure. When a dispute between brethren could not be amicably settled by them, the matter should be decided before *the saints*, the church [cf *Matt* 18:17]' (Norman Hillyer).

*V*2 : **Or know ye not that the saints shall judge the world ? and if the world is judged by you, are ye unworthy to judge the smallest matters ?**

Or know ye not ? The fact that this question is repeated no less than six times within a few verses gives some indication of the strength of Paul's feeling [cf *vv* 3, 9, 15, 16, 19]. He administers this stinging rebuke because their conduct fell far short of their knowledge. Evidently they had been taught that the saints would be associated with Christ in the judgment of the world [cf *Dan* 7:22], and yet they had fallen so far beneath their dignity as to call for the arbitration of heathen magistrates ! It was a shameful absurdity that those who were destined to judge the world should now confess their incompetence to decide even the smallest matters pertaining to the present age [*v* 3]. 'This office the saints will hold by virtue of their perfected knowledge, their completed communion with the judgments of the Great Judge. This is a necessary part of the ultimate triumph of good over evil. Just as the faithful shall reign with Christ as kings [2 *Tim* 2:12; *Rev* 22:5], so shall they sit with Him as judges of the world. The thought is an extension of the promise made to the Apostles [*Matt* 19:28; *Luke* 22:30]: comp. *Rev* 20:4' (Lightfoot).

V3 : Know ye not that we shall judge angels? how much more, things that pertain to this life?

These must be 'the angels which kept not their first estate' [*Jude* 6], for there is no mention in Scripture of a judgment of the elect angels. But the omission of the article before the word 'angels' shows that it does not fall within the scope of the apostle's present purpose to specify the class of angels to be judged. 'Paul does not mean to designate these or those angels; he wishes to awaken within the church the feeling of its competency and dignity by reminding it that beings of so exalted a nature shall one day be subjected to its jurisdiction' (Godet).

How much more, matters pertaining to this life! (RSV) It is better to understand this as a concluding exclamation rather than a further question, because it expresses more forcibly the tremendous contrast between mundane affairs and supernatural beings.

V4 : If then ye have to judge things pertaining to this life, do ye set them to judge who are of no account in the church?

If this is understood as a question, then Paul is drawing attention to the incongruity of appealing to those who are 'of no account in the church', i.e. heathen judges. But it is most unlikely that the apostle would apply such a strong phrase to the civil power without further explanation [cf *Rom* 13:1f], and it is therefore preferable to take it as a command: 'set them to judge who are least esteemed in the church' (AV). Paul's tone is sarcastic. 'Since you are to take part in the future judgment of the world, it ought not to be beyond the present capacity of your least *gifted* (and so least esteemed) members to decide such trifling matters among you!' As Edwards remarks, 'He is not justifying their contempt of brethren, but stating it, and in stating it, really rebuking their pride'.

V5: **I say *this* to move you to shame. What, cannot there be *found* among you one wise man who shall be able to decide between his brethren,**
V6: **but brother goeth to law with brother, and that before unbelievers?**

'If false pride had not made you blind to your real shame, it would not have been necessary for me to write in this ironical vein' [*v* 4]. Paul was not seriously urging the Corinthians to conduct a protracted judicial enquiry, for he regarded such litigation as being quite out of place among brethren. 'Are you then saying, by thus appealing to the judgment of heathen courts, that after all your pretentious claims to wisdom there is not even *one* wise man to be found among you, who shall be able to settle differences between one brother and another?'

and that before unbelievers? 'This is the climax. That there should be disputes about "ordinary matters" is bad; that Christian should go to law with Christian is worse; that Christians should do this before unbelievers is worst of all. It is a scandal before the heathen world' (Robertson – Plummer).

V7: **Nay, already it is altogether a defect in you, that ye have lawsuits one with another. Why not rather take wrong? why not rather be defrauded?**
V8: **Nay, but ye yourselves do wrong, and defraud, and that *your* brethren.**

'In fact before you reach the court, this is altogether a loss, *an utter defeat for you*!' (Arndt-Gingrich). 'You trust to overreach, to gain a victory: it is really a loss, a defeat, before the trial even comes on' (Lightfoot). It is not by engaging in internecine strife and inflicting such grievous wounds upon themselves that the real victory is to be won, but by enduring the wrong and patiently waiving their 'rights' [13:4; *Matt* 5:39, 40). In *v* 8 Paul contrasts their Christian obligation with the sad fact of their lovelessness. Far from being willing to submit to wrong, they actually inflict it, and that on their brethren !

*V*9: **Or know ye not that the unrighteous shall not inherit the kingdom of God? Be not deceived: neither fornicators, nor idolaters, nor adulterers, nor effeminate, nor abusers of themselves with men,**
*V*10: **nor thieves, nor covetous, nor drunkards, nor revilers, nor extortioners, shall inherit the kingdom of God.**

The suffering without rebuke of those who were guilty of wronging their brethren in this way proved that the Corinthians had forgotten an elementary truth. This is now brought home to their conscience in the emphatic assertion that '*wrong-doers*' will not inherit *God's* kingdom. The juxtaposition of the italicized words manifests the absurdity of entertaining such an expectation. Yet the danger of their remaining under the spell of this delusion is underlined by the imperative: 'Be not deceived'. If they really thought that gospel liberty was to be equated with lawless licence, then they had better think again. For as righteousness is the fundamental characteristic of God's kingdom, so those whose lives are still characterized by unrighteousness cannot hope to acquire an interest in that kingdom. Paul knows nothing of a mere interim-ethic, an ethical norm which pertains only to the present life, for in fact the 'ethics of the kingdom yet to come determine the morals of the kingdom that now is' (Edwards). He goes on to define the unrighteousness which debars men from any share in the heavenly inheritance in a representative list of sins, each one of which is a violation of the moral law as set forth in the decalogue. It is because this law expresses the divine standard of righteousness that the infringement of any one of its precepts must result in the exclusion of the transgressor from the kingdom of God. This therefore serves to demonstrate the abiding validity of the moral law, and the permanent obligation of all believers to obey it; no longer to secure their justification, but to give evidence of it. 'The law sends us to the gospel for our justification; the gospel sends us to the law to frame our way of life. . . Christ has freed us from the *manner* of our obedience, but not from the *matter* of our obedience' (Samuel Bolton, *The True Bounds of Christian Freedom*, p. 72). But as for fornicators, idolaters, adulterers, homosexuals (literally: 'catamites' and 'sodomites'), thieves, the covetous, drunkards, revilers, extortioners – *none* of these shall inherit God's kingdom!

*V*11: **And such were some of you: but ye were washed, but ye were sanctified, but ye were justified in the name of the Lord Jesus Christ, and in the Spirit of our God.**

And such were some of you: All the Corinthians were sinners in need of salvation, but only some of them had been guilty of such gross sins. The emphasis falls on the fact that all this now lies in the past; you *were* once like that, but by the grace of God you are so no longer [cf *Eph* 2:11–13].

but ye had yourselves washed, The verb is in the middle voice and refers to baptism 'in its spiritual meaning; the form of the verb calls attention to the initiative of the Corinthians in getting rid, at the call of God, of the filth of their old life; in baptism their penitent faith took deliberate and formal expression, with this effect' (Findlay). [Acts 22:16; 1 Pet 3:21]

but ye were sanctified, but ye were justified Both these verbs direct attention to the action of God which gave their baptism its objective significance. It is not therefore the process of sanctification that is in view. 'Ye were sanctified' means: 'It was then that God claimed you for his own and conferred upon you the status of saints'. Paul puts this before 'ye were justified' because he wishes to stress the act of consecration which had separated them from their former sinful course of self-pleasing. But the latter remains the ground of this consecration, for only those whom God declares just are truly holy.

in the name of the Lord Jesus Christ, and in the Spirit of our God. 'In the name' is the external essential, as 'in the Spirit' is the internal essential of Christian baptism (Lightfoot). C. K. Barrett notes the 'quite unconscious Trinitarianism of the concluding words': *the Lord Jesus Christ, the Spirit, our God.* This is the faith that is confessed throughout the New Testament, for whether 'God is thought of in himself or in his operations, the underlying conception runs unaffectedly into trinal forms' (B. B. Warfield, *Biblical and Theological Studies*, p. 49).

*V*12: **All things are lawful for me; but not all things are expedient. All things are lawful for me; but I will not be brought under the power of any.**

Apparently while Paul was at Corinth he had asserted the freedom of believers from the restrictions of the ceremonial law in the maxim: 'All things are lawful for me', to which some were now appealing to justify their moral laxity. It is because he does not seek to curb licence by a relapse into legalism that he refuses to retract the principle, though he guards against its further abuse by a double qualification. Thus in upholding his doctrine of liberty, while refusing to minister to licence, Paul here presents in germ a complete Christian ethic, which is 'anti-libertine without being legalistic' (Jean Héring).

"All things are lawful for me," but not all things are helpful. (RSV) I. The Christian has the liberty to refrain from indulging in those things which are not spiritually helpful to him. 'This gives the *self-regarding*, as 10:23f the *other-regarding* rule of Christian temperance in the use of things lawful' (Findlay).

"All things are lawful for me," but I will not be enslaved by anything. (RSV) 2. The Christian has the duty of abstaining from those things which would deprive him of his liberty. 'The reasonable use of my liberty cannot go the length of involving my own loss if it, or of rendering me a slave by reducing me to a thing' (Godet).

*V*13: **Meats for the belly, and the belly for meats: but God shall bring to nought both it and them. But the body is not for fornication, but for the Lord; and the Lord for the body:**

"Food is meant for the stomach and the stomach for food" – and God will destroy both one and the other. (RSV) The libertines in Corinth were evidently using this as a slogan to show that sensual indulgence was as natural and necessary to the body, as food was to the stomach. 'If I may gratify one bodily appetite, why may I not gratify another?' (Robertson – Plummer). Paul agrees that food is in itself (*not* as it is offered to idols, ch 8; 10:25f) a matter which is morally indifferent [*Mark* 7:15-23]. According to its present constitution the body certainly needs food to nourish it, but God has no permanent plans for the stomach! There is a time coming when the body will neither need food, nor the organs to digest it.

But the body is not for fornication, but for the Lord; and the Lord for the body: This explains why the supposed analogy between food and fornication does not hold good. Since the Greeks tended to think of the body as the temporary prison or tomb of the soul, they could regard the acts of the body as having no necessary connection with the soul's immortal destiny. But according to the biblical teaching man is a living unity of body and soul – a view which has been emphatically endorsed by modern medicine – and there is therefore no basis for maintaining that physical acts are morally indifferent. Paul here teaches that the body as a whole, in contrast to its temporary apparatus, is fashioned for the Lord's use. Hence to yield it to harlotry is to deny Christ's rights in it and disqualify oneself for a part in his resurrection [*v* 14]. The Lord Jesus and 'fornication' contested for 'the bodies of Christian men; loyal to him they must renounce *that*, yielding to *that* they renounce him' (Findlay).

*V*14: **and God both raised the Lord, and will raise up us through his power.**

Paul will later deal at length with Corinthian doubts about the resurrection [ch 15]; here he simply affirms that the body unlike its perishable members [*v* 13], has a glorious destiny. 'As God raised up Christ, he will also raise the body which has become here below the property and sanctified organ of Christ. The apostle says, "will raise *us* also"; he thus expressly identifies our personality with the body which is to be its eternal organ' (Godet). [*Rom* 8-11; *Phil* 3:21]

*V*15: **Know ye not that your bodies are members of Christ? shall I then take away the members of Christ, and make them members of a harlot? God forbid.**

The repeated question again implies that the Corinthians were not ignorant of the fact, but were far from realizing its implications [cf 12:12-27; *Rom* 12:5]. For if the whole body belongs to the Lord [*v* 13], then how can *I* possibly unite its members with those of a harlot? Paul speaks to them in these realistic terms in order to bring home the enormity of the sin, while 'God forbid' expresses his personal revulsion against the infamy of such a proposal.

*V*16: **Or know ye not that he that is joined to a harlot is one body? for, The twain, saith he, shall become one flesh.**

Paul here teaches the promiscuous Corinthians that there is no such thing as casual sex, because the very nature of the sexual act means that the partners become one body. According to Scripture 'this union is more than an incidental function of the members. It is a coming together as one *body*, and it is thus of far-reaching significance for the whole physico-spiritual personal life' (J. Horst, *TDNT*, Vol. IV, p. 565). The quotation of God's ordinance [*Gen* 2:26] at once confirms and serves to advance Paul's argument, for in this context the transition from the ethically neutral word 'body' to 'flesh' is an eloquent reminder of our fallen condition.

*V*17: **But he that is joined unto the Lord is one spirit.**

As he who joins himself to a harlot is one *flesh* with her, so he who is joined to the Lord becomes one *spirit* with him. Paul speaks of a voluntary attachment which in one case leads to the ultimate degradation, and in the other promotes the highest exaltation, of the human personality. He omits the article before the word 'spirit' in order to contrast it with 'flesh' in the preceding verse, but such a union with Christ presupposes the supernatural work of the Holy Spirit to effect it.

*V*18: **Flee fornication. Every sin that a man doeth is without the body; but he that committeth fornication sinneth against his own body.**

Flee fornication. As the danger is ever-present, the command is in the present tense. 'Other vices are overcome by resistance [cf *Eph* 6:13; *James* 4:7]. The imagination detracts from the fascination of other sins, but adds fuel to the flame of fleshly lusts. . . Perhaps the close connection in Corinth between impurity and idolatry caused the apostle to give the same warning in reference to idolatry also [cf 10:14]' (Edwards). [*Gen* 39:12]

. . . but he that committeth fornication sinneth against his own body. Although sins like drunkenness and gluttony are an *abuse* of the body, whose harmful effects it is every man's duty to foresee and avoid, they are still introduced *from without.* 'But fornication is the *alienating of that body which is the Lord's, and making it a harlot's body* – it is sin *against a man's own body,* in its very nature, – against *the verity and nature* of his body; not an *effect on* the body from participation of things without, but a *contradiction of the truth* of the body, wrought *within itself.* When *man* and *wife* are one in the Lord – united *by his ordinance,* – no such alienation of the body takes place, and consequently no sin' (Alford). [*Prov* 6:30–32; 7:6–27]

*V*19: **Or know ye not that your body is a temple of the Holy Spirit which is in you, which ye have from God? and ye are not your own;**

Or know ye not that your body is a sanctuary of the

Holy Spirit which is in you, (ASV margin) Because each believer is indwelt by the Holy Spirit his body is a veritable sanctuary of God, which must not be dishonoured by the foul sin of fornication. 'The Christian estimate of fornication is thus categorically opposed to the heathen estimate. In the temple of Aphrodite prostitutes were priestesses, and commerce with them was counted a *consecration*; it is an absolute *desecration* of God's true temple in the man himself' (Findlay).

which ye have from God? The phrase is intended 'to emphasize strongly the superhuman origin of that Spirit whom the believer receives, and the dignity of the body in which this Divine Guest comes to dwell' (Godet) [cf 1 *Thess* 4:1-8]

and ye are not your own; 'Since your body is the shrine of the Spirit, the very dwelling place of the Deity, it is no longer yours to command; it belongs to Another and that by right of purchase' [v 20].

*V*20: **for ye were bought with a price: glorify God therefore in your body.**

There may well be an allusion here to the contemporary practice of sacral manumission. Just as a slave gained his freedom by becoming the servant of the god who purchased him, so the readers were released from their slavery to sin in order to serve the new Owner who had bought them. The aorist tense indicates the once-for-all character of this transaction. Thus 'the redeemed are paradoxically slaves, the slaves of God, for they were bought with a price... Believers are not brought by Christ into a liberty of selfish ease. Rather, since they have been bought by God at terrible cost, they have become God's slaves, to do his will' (Leon Morris, *The Apostolic Preaching of the Cross*, p. 54). [7:23; cf *Rom* 6:18, 22]

[96]

glorify God therefore in your body. They must comply with the command at once. They are not merely to abstain from defiling God's sanctuary, but also to render such service *in* it as truly to glorify him whose property it now is by the double right of creation and redemption.

CHAPTER SEVEN

Paul's advice on marriage here begins his reply to the various questions put to him by the Corinthians. Although the unmarried state has its advantages for those who like himself have the gift for it, it is better to marry than to fall into sin. But voluntary asceticism has no place in marriage, which involves the obligation of maintaining normal sexual relations, unless there be a temporary abstention by mutual consent for devotional purposes [vv 1-9]. Since the experience of salvation does not annul the marriage bond, the Christian must stay with the pagan partner who wishes to continue the relationship, for this may lead to the conversion of the unbelieving partner [vv 10-16]. Faith in Christ does not demand a change in their external condition, and so as a general rule, Paul counsels every man to remain in the state in which he was called. Yet if a slave were given the opportunity to gain his freedom, he should take it [vv 17-24]. During the present distress it is good to avoid the added cares of the married state, especially as this course also leaves the individual free to serve the Lord without distraction. But if any father feels ashamed that his daughter is unmarried, he may let her marry. As marriage is dissolved by death, a widow is free to marry again, but only in the Lord [vv 25-40].

*V*1: **Now concerning the things whereof ye wrote: It is good for a man not to touch a woman.**

After having dealt with weightier matters concerning which the Corinthians had not deemed it necessary to ask his advice, Paul is now willing to answer a number of questions on which they had sought his guidance in their letter to him [cf 7:25, 8:1, 12:1, 16:1]. He begins with the subject of marriage because it is closely connected with the previous warning against fornication. What follows is a specific reply to particular problems, and is not an exhaustive statement of his teaching on marriage [cf *Eph* 5:22-33]. His discussion of these problems is not at all tentative, but completely authoritative as befits an apostle of Jesus Christ.

It is good for a man not to touch a woman. If this is not a quotation from the Corinthians' letter, it at least appears to represent what was put to Paul in it. But as in 6:12, he repeats the claim only in order to qualify it. He is not saying that celibacy is morally superior to marriage, but that it is commendable in those who have the special gift for it. All such are free wholly to devote themselves to the service of the Lord [*v* 32], but if celibacy is good, marriage is natural. It would seem that the licence of some in Corinth had provoked others to the opposite extreme of asceticism. However, as will immediately appear, Paul is no more willing to brand the conjugal relation as unlawful than he was prepared to admit the lawfulness of fornication.

*V*2: **But, because of fornications, let each man have his own wife, and let each woman have her own husband.**

'But' places a limitation on the preceding statement. Although celibacy is good, it is not expedient in a city so dissolute as Corinth where the temptation to sin abounds. Here the plural 'fornications' points to the variety and extent of its profligacy. In the light of this situation the apostle not merely recommends the unmarried to marry, but positively

[99]

commands it. Moreover, the form in which the command is expressed at once sanctions monogamy and forbids polygamy. 'Paul does not lay down here the *ground* of marriage, as though it were "ordained for a remedy against sin", but gives a special reason why those should marry at Corinth who might otherwise have remained single' (Findlay).

***V3*: Let the husband render unto the wife her due: and likewise also the wife unto the husband.**

***V4*: The wife hath not power over her own body, but the husband: and likewise also the husband hath not power over his own body, but the wife.**

The fact that Paul uses the present imperative in verse 3 shows that he regards the mutual recognition of conjugal rights as the normal condition of married life. 'It is not the conferring of a favour, but the payment of a debt' (Robertson–Plummer). For since husband and wife are one flesh, neither has the right to refuse intercourse with the other. Paul insists upon the reciprocal nature of the married relation: '*she* is as much the mistress of his person, as *he* the master of hers' (Findlay).

***V5*: Defraud ye not one the other, except it be by consent for a season, that ye may give yourselves unto prayer, and may be together again, that Satan tempt you not because of your incontinency.**

The command 'Defraud ye not' implies that some in Corinth were mistakenly reacting to the sexual vices of their pagan neighbours by practising asceticism within marriage. But Paul, who never falls into the error of countering one evil by endorsing another, will have none of these 'spiritual' unions. 'The apostle teaches that neither party has the right to separate from the other; that no separation is to be allowed which is not with mutual consent, for a limited time, for the purpose of special devotion, and with the definite intention of reunion. Nothing can be more foreign to the mind of the apostle than the spirit which filled the monasteries and convents of the mediaeval church' (Hodge).

that Satan tempt you not because of your incontinency. It is because Paul recognizes that married people are 'incontinent'–for they would have remained unmarried if they had been devoid of sexual desire–that he recommends the regular payment of these marital dues as the best protection against the temptations of Satan. 'Therefore, those who give up intercourse are acting thoughtlessly, indeed as if they had made an arrangement with God for perpetual power of resistance' (Calvin).

*V*6: **But this I say by way of concession, not of commandment.**

What Paul allows by way of concession is not the resumption of intercourse, but its suspension for a limited period. In marriage sexual relations are the norm, and the only ascetic restraint which he permits (but refuses to impose) is 'this' temporary abstinence for devotional purposes [*v* 5].

*V*7: **Yet I would that all men were even as I myself. Howbeit each man hath his own gift from God, one after this manner, and another after that.**

Paul wishes that all were even as he was himself, *viz.* that they possessed the same gift of continence which enabled him to remain unmarried, for then they too could devote themselves entirely to the Lord's service [*v* 32; cf *Matt* 19:11, 12]. However, he freely acknowledges that not all have received this special gift from God, and those who have not must marry. The second part of the verse does not mean that marriage is also one of God's charismatic gifts; it is a creation ordinance which requires no special gift of grace. 'What

Paul means is that one Christian has a special gift from God in one direction, another in an entirely different direction. Grace works in all manner of directions as Paul shows *in extenso* in 1 *Cor* 12:8, etc.' (Lenski).

*V*8: **But I say to the unmarried and to widows, It is good for them if they abide even as I.**

Paul here expresses his conviction that it is good (or to use Edwards' phrase 'morally beautiful') for the unmarried (including the widows who might well wish for a change in their sad lot) to remain as they are; he insists that no stigma is attached to the single state [*v* 1].

if they abide even as I. Paul is unmarried (though he may have been a widower, or perhaps was even deserted by his wife after his conversion, cf. *v* 15). He has made his own decision, and he is persuaded that others would do well to follow his example, but significantly he leaves the choice open to them. There is no command or even a hint of constraint in the clause.

*V*9: **But if they have not continency, let them marry: for it is better to marry than to burn.**

This gives evidence of Paul's clear-sighted realism. Those who lack the gift of continency will be unable to acquire it, and so he directs them to marry rather than burn with unsatisfied desire [*v* 2]. 'Enforced abstinence is valueless if it means being *aflame with passion*, *i.e.* emotionally distracted by unsatisfied appetite. Sexual desire is natural and marriage is provided for its fulfilment' (Hillyer).

*V*10: **But unto the married I give charge, *yea* not I, but the Lord, That the wife depart not from her husband**
*V*11: **(but should she depart, let her remain unmarried,**

or else be reconciled to her husband); and that the husband leave not his wife.

Ordinarily, Paul writes on his own authority as an inspired apostle[14:37], but here he appeals to the direct ruling of the Lord himself [*Mark* 10:9, 11, 12]. As the wife is not to leave home, so the husband is not to send her away from it. 'The sense of the double command is that neither a Christian wife nor a Christian husband should disrupt and thus destroy the marriage in which they are joined' (Lenski). Having entered into a permanent bond, it is not open to either partner to settle disagreements by resorting to divorce. Fornication is not mentioned because that would dissolve the marriage relationship [*Matt* 5:32]. But if, in spite of the command, the wife should desert her husband she is not free to remarry while he lives [*Rom* 7:3], and must either remain as she is, or else be reconciled to her husband. 'No one will say that such a case was not likely to occur in the Corinthian church, who bears in mind the ease with which a divorce was obtainable in Greece or Rome' (Edwards).

*V*12: **But to the rest say I, not the Lord: If any brother hath an unbelieving wife, and she is content to dwell with him, let him not leave her.**
*V*13: **And the woman that hath an unbelieving husband, and he is content to dwell with her, let her not leave her husband.**

Paul deals next with the problem of those who became Christians after their marriage and now had a heathen partner [*vv* 12-16]. His first direction is that such unions are not to be terminated on the initiative of the believing partner. If it is now a *mixed* marriage, it is nevertheless still a *marriage*, and provided the unbeliever is content to live under these changed circumstances then the relationship must be continued. With those who are already Christians before marriage the case is entirely different; they are to marry 'only in the Lord' [*v* 39].

say I, not the Lord: It is noteworthy that though Paul carefully distinguishes between his own words and those of the Lord he regards both as equally authoritative [cf *v* 10 with *v* 17]. The 'contrast is not between the inspired teaching of Christ and the uninspired teaching of the apostle but rather between the teaching of the apostle that could appeal to the express utterances of Christ in the days of his flesh, on the one hand, and the teaching of the apostle that went beyond the cases dealt with by Christ, on the other. There is no distinction as regards the binding character of the teaching in these respective cases' (John Murray, *The Infallible Word*, p. 38).

*V*14: **For the unbelieving husband is sanctified in the wife, and the unbelieving wife is sanctified in the brother: else were your children unclean; but now are they holy.**

Instead of becoming defiled by remaining married to an unbeliever, the holiness of the Christian partner in such a match actually serves to 'sanctify' (i.e. bring within the sphere of spiritual blessing) the unbelieving spouse. 'He stands upon the sacred threshold of the church: his *surroundings* are hallowed. United to a saintly consort, he is in daily contact with saintly conduct: holy association may become holy assimilation, and the sanctity which ever environs may at last penetrate. But the man's *conversion* is not a condition necessary to the sanctity of the subsisting conjugal union' (T. S. Evans cited in Robertson-Plummer).

else were your children unclean; but now are they holy. Unless the marriage were thus 'sanctified', their children would be ritually unclean, but as matters stand they are 'holy'. Since the holiness of the children is not inferred from the faith of the believing parent, but from the sanctification of the unbelieving party, it follows 'that the holiness of the children cannot be superior, either as to nature or degree, to that sanctification of the unbelieving partner from which it is derived' (T. E. Watson, *Baptism not for Infants*, p. 39). Hence if the possession of this 'holiness' authorizes the baptism of infants, then the unbelieving parent through whom it was bestowed would be equally eligible to receive it!

*V*15: **Yet if the unbelieving departeth, let him depart: the brother or the sister is not under bondage in such** *cases*: **but God hath called us in peace.**

On the other hand, if the unbeliever 'is bent on departing', then 'let him begone' (Edwards). With the departure of the unbelieving spouse the marriage ceases to exist, and in such cases the Christian brother or sister is not 'under bondage'. As the desertion of the unconverted partner effectively dissolves the marriage contract, the apostle must mean that the believer is no longer bound by it, and is therefore free to remarry. This further ground for divorce is known as the 'Pauline privilege' (cf. *The New Bible Dictionary*, p. 790). **but God hath called us in peace.** Or as C. F. D. Moule suggests: *God has called you* **into** *a peace* **in** *which he wishes you to live*. This peace covers both the case of the believer whose partner is content to remain, and of the believer who makes no attempt to force an unwilling partner to stay.

*V*16: **For how knowest thou, O wife, whether thou shalt save thy husband? or how knowest thou, O husband, whether thou shalt save thy wife?**

Paul's meaning is a matter of debate, but in view of the fact that he has already referred to the 'sanctity' of such mixed marriages [*v* 14], it is preferable to take these questions in an optimistic sense (as in the NEB). Paul is thus encouraging the

hope that the living testimony of the Christian wife or husband may lead to the conversion of the pagan partner.

*V*17: **Only, as the Lord hath distributed to each man, as
God hath called each, so let him walk. And so ordain
I in all the churches.**

This 'states the general principle which determines these
questions about marriage, and this is afterwards illustrated
by the cases of circumcision and slavery' (Robertson-Plummer). 'Only' puts limitation on what Paul has just said in
verse 15, for Christian liberty is not social anarchy and must
not be confused with mere change for change's sake. Hence the
apostle insists that every believer's daily walk is to be regulated
by two considerations: 1. That every circumstance in life
is governed by the glorified Christ; 2. That he is to remain
in that station which was his when God called him to salvation. 'Paul does not mean to stereotype a Christian's
secular employment from the time of his conversion, but
forbids his renouncing this under a false notion of spiritual
freedom, or in contempt of secular things as though there
were no will of God for him in their disposition' (Findlay).

And so ordain I in all the churches. 'That is, this is the
rule or order which I lay down in all churches. The apostles,
in virtue of their plenary inspiration, were authorized not
only to teach the doctrines of the gospel, but also to regulate
all matters relating to practice' (Hodge).

*V*18: **Was any man called being circumcised? let him not
become uncircumcised. Hath any been called in uncircumcision? let him not be circumcised.**
*V*19: **Circumcision is nothing, and uncircumcision is
nothing; but the keeping of the commandments of God.**

If a man is called by God it is of no consequence whether

he is a Jew or a Gentile. If he is a Jew, let him not try to become a Gentile by seeking 'to remove the marks of circumcision' [RSV: cf I *Macc* 1:15]; if he is a Gentile, let him not think that he must become a Jew by capitulating to the demands of Judaizers (cf the fiery polemic of *Gal* 5:2ff). A man's state by birth and inheritance has no bearing on his standing before God, and so he should remain as he is. Under the gospel such externals are of no moment, but the doing of God's will is everything! Lightfoot remarks that those who would contrast the teaching of Paul with that of James, 'or who would exaggerate his doctrine of justification by faith, should reflect on this *keeping of the commandments of God*' [cf 9:20f; *Gal* 5:6, 6:15].

*V*20: **Let each man abide in that calling wherein he was called.**

Everyone is to remain in the station in which he found himself when he was called. (Arndt-Gingrich) Paul here emphatically repeats the principle laid down in verse 17. God's summons to salvation does not overthrow the existing social order, but it gradually leavens the lump through the influence of changed lives. The divine call is not to a new 'vocation'; it rather gives the old job a new meaning (though of course a sinful livelihood would have to be renounced, e.g. *Eph* 4:28). 'To be a Christian is not something static, but something dynamic. It is to remain one who is called, to abide in that calling wherewith one is called not once, but always. It is always to hear the voice of God from heaven, which calls men to Christ and away from sin and ungodliness' (Grosheide).

*V*21: **Wast thou called being a bondservant? care not for it: nay, even if thou canst become free, use *it* rather.**

Paul's point is that a man's social position has no bearing

upon his acceptance within the community of faith [cf 1:26]. Hence the converted slave is called to live as a Christian without being troubled if his emancipation from the slavery of sin brings no improvement of his earthly lot.

But if you can gain your freedom, avail yourself of the opportunity. (RSV) But there will be exceptions to this general rule, and the slave who has the opportunity to gain his freedom should take it. Although it is difficult to understand how the author of the Epistle to Philemon could have offered any other advice, many have taken the words in the opposite sense (e.g. Goodspeed: 'Even if you can gain your freedom, make the most of your present condition [as a slave] instead').

*V*22: **For he that was called in the Lord being a bond-servant, is the Lord's freedman: likewise he that was called being free, is Christ's bondservant.**

Since most of those slaves who had been called to faith in Christ would not be offered the opportunity envisaged in *v* 21b, the thought of *v* 21a is resumed to show why the Christian bondservant should be content with his lot. For though he is still a slave in the eyes of men, he is in a spiritual sense the Lord's freedman. 'A double process is indicated here. Christ first buys us from our old master, sin, and then sets us free. For this enfranchisement see *Rom* 8:2, *Gal* 5:1. But observe that a service is still due from the *libertus* to his *patronus*. This was the case in Roman Law, which required the freedman to take his patron's name, live in his patron's house, consult his patron's will, etc.' (Lightfoot).

likewise he that was called being free, is Christ's bondservant. In each case the paradoxical language points to the same spiritual result, and must mean that freedman and slave stand on the same level before Christ. This is because the free man is in bondage to sin until grace makes him the bondservant of Christ. So 'in effect freedom in Christ and slavery to Christ merely represent two sides of the same moral truth: for subjection to Christ is freedom from sin [*Rom* 6:18, 22]' (Lightfoot).

*V*23: **Ye were bought with a price; become not bondservants of men.**

This change to the second person plural shows that Paul now addresses, not just slaves and free men, but the whole church. 'That they have been bought with a price is the proof that they are both the bondmen and the freedmen of Christ. Liberty and service are but the opposite sides of the same fact; for both begin in redemption' (Edwards). [cf 6:20]

become not bondservants of men. The precept implies that such servitude to men is abnormal since it infringes the rights of their divine Owner [*Lev* 25:42, 55]. The Corinthians would revert to this condition of bondage if they allowed worldly modes of thought to determine their attitude to slavery and freedom, circumcision and uncircumcision, marriage and celibacy, or any other social relation. They have been called to Christian freedom, and not to some form of revolutionary emancipation which would be an enslavement rather than a liberation. It was not through the preaching of a 'social' or 'political' gospel that slavery was finally banished from the ancient world, for these 'worldly' messages lack the spiritual dynamic which alone can change the hearts of men and make them truly free.

*V*24: **Brethren, let each man, wherein he was called, therein abide with God.**

The instruction is given for the third time [*vv* 17, 20], yet

Paul never indulges in merely sterile repetition. His discussion of this principle is rounded off with the significant addition: 'therein abide with God'. 'The principal idea is not that of abiding *before God* in that state; it is abiding *in that state*, and that *before God*. By these last words, Paul reminds his readers of the moral act which has the power of sanctifying and ennobling every external position: the eye fixed on God, *walking* in his presence. This is what preserves the believer from the temptations arising from the situation in which he is; this is what raises the humblest duties it can impose on him to the supreme dignity of acts of worship' (Godet).

V25: **Now concerning virgins I have no commandment of the Lord: but I give my judgment, as one that hath obtained mercy of the Lord to be trustworthy.**

On the question of virgins Paul has no command from the Lord, nor does he give a definite directive on the matter himself, because in this case neither alternative is sinful. It is not sinful for a virgin to marry and it is not sinful for her to remain single. Therefore he gives instead his *inspired* advice as 'one that hath obtained mercy of the Lord to be trustworthy', i.e. it is a judgment delivered in the faithful discharge of his commission as an apostle of the Lord Jesus Christ [1 *Tim* 1:12, 13]. 'On certain details of life and behaviour the Lord has not bound us by *law* to one course of action rather than another. If we follow one course rather than the other we have not sinned because we have not transgressed law' (John Murray, *Principles of Conduct*, p. 71). [1 *John* 3 :4]

V26: **I think therefore that this is good by reason of the distress that is upon us, *namely*, that it is good for a man to be as he is.**

Paul begins by declaring his reason for preferring the single state. He thinks that it is good for a person (man or woman) to remain unmarried in view of 'the impending distress' (Arndt-Gingrich). 'The days of the extensive pagan persecutions were drawing nigh. A girl that married and reared a family might thus be doubly and trebly overwhelmed, for her beloved husband might become involved, or she with him—and what about the children? History records many agonizing cases. Paul thus very properly writes that, in the face of the situation prevailing at that time, "a person" may well prefer to remain alone, untrammelled by tender family ties' (Lenski).

*V*27: **Art thou bound unto a wife? seek not to be loosed. Art thou loosed from a wife? seek not a wife.**

'Marriage, in the present circumstances of the church, will prove a burden. Although this fact will not justify the dissolution of any marriage, it should dissuade Christians from getting married' (Hodge).

*V*28: **But shouldest thou marry, thou hast not sinned; and if a virgin marry, she hath not sinned. Yet such shall have tribulation in the flesh: and I would spare you.**

The assurance given here would be inexplicable unless there were some at Corinth who held that marriage was sinful. Paul emphatically rejects this ascetic claim. There is no sin in marrying, but those who marry will find that it involves physical distress, and he would spare them this unnecessary suffering. 'The case of virgins is associated with that of others, in order to show that really there is no difference between them. If virgins sin in marrying, so does a man; if it is because of the impending distress that it is well for all to abstain from marriage, it is well for virgins to do so for the same reason' (Edwards).

*V*29: **But this I say, brethren, the time is shortened, that henceforth both those that have wives may be as though they had none;**

What Paul is about to say applies to all his readers whether married or unmarried. 'But, though I counsel none to change their state, I do counsel all to change their *attitude towards* all earthly things' (Robertson-Plummer).

the time is shortened, The reference is to the Second Advent, not to its chronological nearness, but to the special character which the certainty of this event gives to the period which immediately precedes it. 'The underlying idea is none other than that the times preceding the parousia require a unique concentration of the minds of believers upon the Lord and the manner in which they may best please him. The last days are to be days of undivided and most assiduous interest in the Lord and the unparalleled mode in which he may soon come to reveal himself' (G. Vos, *The Pauline Eschatology*, p. 87).

that henceforth both those that have wives may be as though they had none; These words 'must not be taken as an exhortation to neglect marital duties, as the context clearly shows. They imply that it should be constantly kept in mind that marriage is something of this time, not of the proper abiding life of the Christian' (Grosheide). [*Mark* 12:25]

*V*30: **and those that weep, as though they wept not; and those that rejoice, as though they rejoiced not; and those that buy, as though they possessed not;**

'Sorrows and joys alike are temporary, are transient. In a moment all may be changed. Therefore to one who judges rightly, earthly grief is not over-grievous and earthly joy not over-joyous' (Lightfoot).

as though they possessed not; Although the Christian not only may but must join with unbelievers in buying from the same market-place [cf 10:25], he differs from them in that he regards earthly goods as a trust and not as his permanent possession [*Luke* 12:19, 20].

*V*31: **and those that use the world, as not using it to the full: for the fashion of this world passeth away.**

It is because the unbeliever has no higher expectation that he uses the world to the full, but the believer's hope transcends the world and so he is to look upon all temporal things with a sense of spiritual detachment. 'Home with its joys and griefs, business, the use of the world, must be carried on as under notice to quit, by men prepared to cast loose from the shores of time [cf *Luke* 12:29-36; by contrast, *Luke* 14:18ff]' (Findlay).

for the fashion of this world passeth away. The fascination of the world 'is that of the theatre; but its unreal nature betrays itself in the shifting of the scenes. He appeals to their own observation: "For behold how the scene changes!" Every change proves that the end will come' (Edwards). Therefore, as 'this world in its present form is passing away' (Arndt-Gingrich), believers must not set their hearts upon it, but rather live in the light of its forthcoming transformation [*Rom* 8:19-23; *2 Pet* 3:13].

*V*32: **But I would have you to be free from cares. He that is unmarried is careful for the things of the Lord, how he may please the Lord:**
*V*33: **but he that is married is careful for the things of the world, how he may please his wife,** *v* 34: **and is divided.**

Paul would free the Corinthians from worldly cares so that

they might care for the work of the Lord. The unmarried man is free to engage in this work without distraction, but he who is married must also seek to please his wife 'and is divided'. No reproach is implied; he is simply stating a fact. However, as F. W. Grosheide points out, the absolute statements of *v* 32-34 are not meant to be taken in an absolute sense. They only serve to show that married people are necessarily and properly so much occupied with the affairs of this world that they cannot fix their minds on the Lord's service with the same single-minded intensity that an unmarried person is able to bring to it.

*V*34b: *So* **also the woman that is unmarried and the virgin is careful for the things of the Lord, that she may be holy both in body and in spirit: but she that is married is careful for the things of the world, how she may please her husband.**

In the same way the married woman has the duty of caring for her husband, whereas the widow or virgin is free to 'be holy both in body and in spirit', i.e. she is able to consecrate herself entirely to the Lord's service. Paul says this to encourage and comfort the single woman, and not to cast any reflection upon the married state. There is no justification for interpreting the phrase in an ascetic sense, as though superior holiness were ensured by sexual abstinence.

*V*35: **And this I say for your own profit; not that I may cast a snare upon you, but for that which is seemly, and that ye may attend upon the Lord without distraction.**

In thus advising the Corinthians of the value of remaining single Paul has nothing but their own spiritual advantage in view. He has no desire to deprive them of their liberty by shutting them up to celibacy. He will not capture them as wild animals are taken by throwing 'a noose' around their necks (ASV margin). His recommendation of the single state is limited to those who have the gift for it; he is far from forbidding marriage [cf vv 5, 9; 1 Tim 4:3].

but for that which is seemly, and that ye may attend upon the Lord without distraction. According to G. G. Findlay, 'seemly' means 'of honourable guise', and covers what belongs 'to the Christian decorum of life'. Paul's language here recalls Luke's account of Martha and Mary [Luke 10:38-42]. As Mary chose the one thing needful, he would have them give their undivided attention to the Lord, instead of being 'distracted' by worldly cares as was Martha.

*V*36: **But if any man thinketh that he behaveth himself unseemly toward his virgin *daughter*, if she be past the flower of her age, and if need so requireth, let him do what he will; he sinneth not; let them marry.**

Paul now answers the question, 'Should a Christian father give his daughter in marriage?' [vv 36-38] He says that the father is to make his decision only after taking into account the needs of his daughter. 'If the virgin daughter has passed the bloom or flower of her age and she feels the constraint or necessity of marriage, then the father may consider himself as acting in an unbecoming, perhaps shameful and perilous, manner with reference to his daughter if he refuses to give her in marriage. In such an event let the father give her in marriage and let the virgin and her suitor marry; the father has done what is proper and no sin is entailed for any of the persons concerned' (John Murray, *Principles of Conduct*, p. 75).

*V*37: **But he that standeth steadfast in his heart, having no necessity, but hath power as touching his own will,**

and hath determined this in his own heart, to keep his own virgin *daughter*, **shall do well.**

But if the father: 1. **standeth steadfast**–being unmoved by the social stigma of his daughter remaining unmarried; 2.

having no necessity–arising from the natural inclination of the daughter to find fulfilment in marriage; 3. **but hath power as touching his own will**–because his daughter's will is not in opposition to his; 4. and so **hath determined this in his own heart, to keep his own virgin daughter**– THEN, having satisfied these conditions, he **shall do well.**

*V*38: **So then both he that giveth his own virgin** *daughter* **in marriage doeth well; and he that giveth her not in marriage shall do better.**

Thus neither father sins, both do well, but one does better in withholding his daughter from marriage. '1. For the better waiting upon God's work without distraction. 2. For the better bearing of persecution' (Trapp).

*V*39: **A wife is bound for so long time as her husband liveth; but if the husband be dead, she is free to be married to whom she will; only in the Lord.**
*V*40: **But she is happier if she abide as she is, after my judgment: and I think that I also have the Spirit of God.**

In conclusion Paul deals with the case of widows. The wife is bound to her husband for as long as he lives, but if he dies she is free to marry again, though only to a fellow-believer in the Lord [2 *Cor* 6:14]. Yet in Paul's judgment she would be happier (in the sense already described: *vv* 28, 34, 35) if she did not marry again. 'There is no inconsistency between this and 1 *Tim* 5:14. The "younger widows" come under the rule given in *v* 9' (Robertson-Plummer).

I think that I also An ironical understatement, which invites those Corinthians who claimed the inspiration of the Spirit for their opinions, to reflect upon the fact that Paul also has reason to know that he has God's Spirit [cf *v* 25].

CHAPTER EIGHT

Another matter on which the Corinthians had asked Paul's advice was the lawfulness of eating meat offered to idols. He begins by reminding them that the exercise of knowledge is limited by the higher claim of love [vv 1-3]. It is true that the eating of such food is a matter of indifference to those who know there is but one God and one Mediator, for heathen idols are nothing [vv 4-6]. But to parade this liberty encourages the weaker brother to sin by indulging in that which his conscience condemns. Therefore Paul would rather refuse any food than cause his brother to stumble [vv 7-13].

*V*1: **Now concerning things sacrificed to idols: We know that we all have knowledge. Knowledge puffeth up, but love edifieth.**

It was virtually impossible for Christians living in a pagan society to avoid all contact with the idolatry which so completely permeated it. Evidently there were those in Corinth who, because of their superior knowledge ('we *know* that an idol is nothing in the world'–v 4), felt quite free to eat meat which had been offered to idols, and even accept invitations to attend banquets held in heathen temples. But the believers whom they regarded as less enlightened than themselves were bound by conscientious scruples and could not allow themselves the same liberty. At the very

CHAPTER 8, VERSE I

outset of Paul's discussion of this question he uses a word
which 'conveys an implicit judgment' (Findlay). He calls it
'the *idol*-sacrifice', whereas the pagan said that it was 'sacrificed to a divinity' (Arndt-Gingrich). **We know that we all
have knowledge.** Paul begins his reply by ironically endorsing another Corinthian slogan: We know that 'we *all*
have knowledge!' But in thus boasting of their knowledge,
the 'strong' had overlooked the effect of their liberated
conduct on those who were 'weak' [cf *v* 7].

Knowledge puffeth up, but love buildeth up. (ASV
margin) Paul has no wish to place a premium on ignorance;
he rather desires to show the Corinthians that the loveless
exercise of knowledge is not constructive but destructive in
its effects [*v* 11]. In stressing the superiority of knowledge
they had failed to appreciate the primacy of love (cf ch.13).
'This love "builds up" or "edifies". Instead of fostering pride
in our hearts and puffing us up, love considers others, aids
them in strengthening their spiritual life and in protecting
it from danger' (Lenski).

*V*2: **If any man thinketh that he knoweth anything,
he knoweth not yet as he ought to know;**

The Corinthian know-alls fancied that they knew what the
less knowledgeable did not understand, but Paul insists that
any man who thinks like that does not yet know as he ought
to know. Although such a man is not devoid of knowledge,
his whole way of knowing is radically defective because he
lacks love [1 *John* 4:8]. For the knowledge which puffs up
is not true knowledge, even though the thing known may be
true in itself. 'Spiritual pride', says W. G. T. Shedd, is 'the
last resort of the Tempter, and whoever is enabled by divine
grace to foil him at this point, will foil him at all points'
('Pride Vitiates Religious Knowledge', *Sermons to the Spiritual
Man*, p. 282).

*V*3: **but if any man loveth God, the same is known by him.**

A Christian is not someone who claims to know God through the power of his own will. The soul does not make its own unassisted ascent to God. On the contrary, it is solely because God (the Object of knowledge) has taken the initiative in electing grace and put forth his saving power that a man is enabled to respond to this prior knowledge in grateful love [cf 13:12; Rom 8:29; Gal 4:9; 2 Tim 2:19]. Thus to know God is to love him, and this is the fruit of his having first loved us [1 John 4:19]. 'Paul would ascribe nothing to human acquisition; religion is a bestowment, not an achievement; our love or knowledge is the reflex of the divine love and knowledge directed toward us' (Findlay).

*V*4: **Concerning therefore the eating of things sacrificed to idols, we know that no idol is** *anything* **in the world, and that there is no God but one.**

Having defined the nature of true spiritual knowledge, Paul resumes the topic introduced in verse 1, and endorses two propositions which were apparently expressed by the Corinthians in their letter to him.

we know that 'there is no such thing as an idol in the world (i.e., an idol has no real existence)' (Arndt-Gingrich) Here the apostle is content to echo the claim that an idol (or rather the imaginary deity it represents) has no real existence; whereas in 10:20 he points out that such deluded worshippers actually sacrifice not to Aphrodite, Serapis, or Aesculapius, but to demons whose existence was all too real.

and that 'there is no God but one'. (RSV) Christians are right in affirming that all the gods of the heathen are nonen-

CHAPTER 8, VERSE 4

tities, nothing but hollow shams without a vestige of reality
[1 Thess 1:9]. 'The *world* reveals the being and power of the
One God [*Rom* 1:20]; idolaters have no living God, but are
without God in the world [*Eph* 2:12]' (Findlay).

V5: **For though there be that are called gods, whether
in heaven or on earth; as there are gods many, and lords
many;**

**For indeed, granting the existence of so-called gods,
whether in heaven or upon earth, as indeed there are
many (such) gods and lords,** (Findlay) Although believers
know that there is only one God, yet in the minds of pagan
worshippers the existence of these false gods is real enough.
But if Paul denies the actual existence of the deities represented
by these idols [*v* 4], he nevertheless admits that behind the
façade of heathen worship there lurked evil powers upon
which it terminated [10:20].

V6: **yet to us there is one God, the Father, of whom
are all things, and we unto him; and one Lord, Jesus
Christ, through whom are all things, and we through
him.**

Yet to us 'To us, Christians, there is but one God and
one Lord. The inference–which the apostle leaves his readers
to draw–is that we, Christians, at least, should not regard
meat offered to an idol as either sanctified or polluted'
(Edwards).

there is one God. . . and one Lord Paul here opposes the
numerous deities and secondary mediators of heathenism
('Gods a-plenty and Lords a-plenty'–Warfield) with the
one *God* [*v* 4], and the one Mediatorial *Lord*, Jesus Christ,
through whom we are brought near to this otherwise
unapproachable God. As in creation all things are *from* the

[121]

Father *through* Christ, so in the new creation all things (and especially the redeemed) are *through* Christ *unto* the Father [2 *Cor* 5:17; *Col* 1:15-22]. When 'Paul says "God the Father and the Lord Jesus Christ", he has in mind not two Gods, much less two beings of unequal dignity, a God and a Demi-god, or a God and a mere creature, – but just one God. Though Christians have one God the Father and one Lord Jesus Christ, they know but one only God' (B. B. Warfield, *Biblical and Theological Studies*, p. 75).

*V*7: **Howbeit there is not in all men that knowledge: but some, being used until now to the idol, eat as *of* a thing sacrificed to an idol; and their conscience being weak is defiled.**

Paul now corrects the assertion of the enlightened: 'We all have knowledge' [*v* 1]. There is not in *all* men that knowledge. Some Gentiles have been so accustomed to regard idols as real that, in spite of their conversion, they still cannot get rid of the feeling that, by eating meat sacrificed to idols, they are participating in the worship of heathen gods. Consequently, when the example of their stronger-minded brethren encourages them to eat such food, they become guilty of doing that which their conscience condemns. For 'whatsoever is not of faith is sin' [*Rom* 14:23].

*V*8: **But food will not commend us to God: neither, if we eat not, are we the worse; nor, if we eat, are we the better.**

But '**food will not bring us before (the judgment seat of) God**': (Arndt-Gingrich) Paul reiterates the conviction of the 'strong' in Corinth and allows its truth. 'Food will not bring us into any relation, good or bad, with God: it will have no effect on the estimate which He will form respecting us, or on the judgment which He will pronounce upon us. It is not one of the things which we shall have to answer for [*Rom* 14:17]. It is the clean heart, and not clean food, that will matter; and the weak brother confounds the two' (Robertson – Plummer).

neither, if we eat not, do we lack; nor, if we eat, do we abound. (ASV margin) 'Not eating leaves us with no deficit that we should deplore, and eating gives us no balance to our credit to which we may point with pride' (Lenski).

*V*9: **But take heed lest by any means this liberty of yours become a stumblingblock to the weak.**

But 'Though food does not affect our relation to God, it may affect our relation to our brethren and so bring us indirectly under the condemnation of God' (Edwards). Therefore love for the brethren must lead the 'strong' to limit this liberty (or right) of theirs, lest by insisting upon their 'rights' ('All things are lawful for me' – 6:12) they should cause the 'weak' to stumble.

*V*10: **For if a man see thee who hast knowledge sitting at meat in an idol's temple, will not his conscience, if he is weak, be emboldened to eat things sacrificed to idols?**

If then a 'weak' brother sees the knowledgeable Christian dining with his heathen friends before the shrine of an idol, will not his conscience 'be builded up to eat things sacrificed to idols?' (ASV margin). The question is ironical. 'Will you "build up" the weak brother by your enlightened example? You will "build him up" by bringing him to ruin!' Here Paul only has in view the evil effects of this example upon others; he later brands the practice as being in itself sinful [10:14ff].

*V*11: **For through thy knowledge he that is weak perisheth, the brother for whose sake Christ died.**

Since Paul speaks of the brother for whom Christ died, it is wrong to assume that 'perisheth' must here signify eternal perdition, for *apollumi* can also refer to temporal loss or ruin (e.g. in *Matt* 9:17 it is used of bursting wineskins; in *Luke* 15:9, 32 of the lost being found; in *Luke* 15:17 of perishing with hunger; and in *James* 1:11 of fading blossoms). Thus the loveless abuse of knowledge results in the 'wounding' [*v* 12] or '*ruining*' of the weak believer–by causing him 'to act against his conscience, and so to commit sin and be in danger of quenching God's Spirit within him' [Alford on *Rom* 14:15].

*V*12: **And thus, sinning against the brethren, and wounding their conscience when it is weak, ye sin against Christ.**

The verse gives a vivid description of the violence inflicted upon the conscience while it is weak and so in no condition to withstand the blow: 'how base to strike the weak!' (Findlay). **ye sin against Christ.** A lesson which Paul himself had been taught by the Risen Christ on the road to Damascus [*Acts* 9:4, 5]. 'The principle of union with Christ, which forbids sin against oneself [6:15], forbids sin against one's brother' (Findlay).

*V*13: **Wherefore, if meat causeth my brother to stumble, I will eat no flesh for evermore, that I cause not my brother to stumble.**

Paul does not specify the kind of meat (in this case: 'meat offered to idols'), because he is stating a principle of universal application which holds good for every kind of eating [cf *Rom* 14:14, 17, 21]. The vehemence of Paul's language expresses the strength of his conviction, yet he does not unconditionally renounce his liberty, but abridges it only in the interests of his brother. And what follows shows the

Corinthians how far he has gone in this regard [p·1ff] 'The strong sought the solution of the question from the standpoint of knowledge and its rights; the apostle finds it from the standpoint of love and its obligations' (C. Holsten).

CHAPTER NINE

Paul answers his critics by affirming that at least the Corinthians have no reason to doubt the reality of his apostleship since they were converted under his ministry [vv 1-3]. And though he had the same right to marry and receive the support of the churches as the other apostles, he had chosen to forego his rights in order to further the gospel by preaching it without charge [vv 4-18]. For though he was free from all men, he curtailed his own liberty by adapting himself to the many he longed to gain for Christ, whether they were Jews, Gentiles, or even the weak! [vv 19-23]. When athletes strive so hard for a corruptible crown, believers must not expect to obtain an incorruptible crown without sacrifice [vv 24-25]. Therefore Paul is always in strict training, lest having preached to others, he should be rejected himself [vv 26, 27].

*V*1: **Am I not free? am I not an apostle? have I not seen Jesus our Lord? are not ye my work in the Lord?**

Paul establishes his credentials as an apostle by asking four rhetorical questions in the familiar debating style of the day (the diatribe), and his use of the negative ('not') implies that the answer he expects to each is 'yes' (W. H. Mare). The *first* question looks back to the previous chapter, and it rebukes those who protest their 'rights' to the ruination of their brothers. As a Christian Paul enjoyed the same freedom as the Corinthians, but in refusing to exercise that liberty to the full in the interests of the weak he exemplified the doctrine he preached.

The *second* question affirms what some were already inclined to deny, for Paul's critics evidently argued that a full apostle would have insisted upon having all his expenses paid by the church. But love's motives are always misunderstood by loveless hearts. Paul was no less an apostle because he had waived what he had every right to demand from them.

The *third* question underlines an essential feature of his apostleship. The fact that Paul has seen 'Jesus our Lord' made him a witness of the resurrection, and the fact that he saw him 'last of all' [15:8] made him the last member of the apostolic college. It was through that encounter with the Risen Christ on the Damascus road that he was called to salvation and commissioned for service [*Gal* 1:15f].

The *fourth* question gives a further proof of his apostleship. The Corinthians were not obliged to believe Paul's testimony that he had seen the Lord as a matter of mere hearsay, since all 'the signs of an apostle' [2 *Cor* 12:12] were wrought in their midst, and indeed their own conversion to Christ afforded the most conspicuous proof of this power!

*V*2: **If to others I am not an apostle, yet at least I am to you; for the seal of mine apostleship are ye in the Lord.**

The Corinthians should have been the very last to dispute Paul's apostleship when they owed their salvation to his work 'in the Lord'. 'The conversion of men is a divine work, and those by whom it is accomplished are thereby authenticated as divine messengers . . . This, although valid evidence, and as such adduced by the apostle, is nevertheless very liable to be abused. First, because much which passes for conversion is spurious; and secondly, because the evidence of success is often urged in behalf of the errors of preachers, when that success is due to the truth which they preach' (Hodge).

for the seal of mine apostleship are ye in the Lord. A seal 'is a visible token of something that already exists; thus the Corinthian church does not make Paul an apostle, and his apostleship does not depend on it (any more than on the Jerusalem church – cf *Gal* 1:1), but its existence is a visible sign of his apostleship' (Barrett). [*Rom* 4:11; 2 *Cor* 1:22]

*V*3 : **My defence to them that examine me is this.**

Opinion is divided on whether 'this' refers to what follows or to what precedes. The latter is perhaps the preferable alternative. '"*This*" – referring to *vv* 1, 2 – "is my answer to those that put me on my defence": I point them to you! . . . Granted the *apostleship* (and this the readers cannot deny), the *right* followed as a matter of course: this needed no "apology"' (Findlay).

*V*4 : **Have we no right to eat and to drink ?**
*V*5 : **Have we no right to lead about a wife that is a believer, even as the rest of the apostles, and the brethren of the Lord, and Cephas ?**

In Corinth Paul had not exercised his right to be supported by the church, but this forbearance did not mean that he had forfeited that right [*Acts* 18:3; 2 *Cor* 12:13-16]. Then again, if Paul were to marry a believing sister and take her with him on his missionary travels as did most of the apostles, he would be entitled to the same support for himself *and his wife* as these married apostles actually received from the churches. He, might well have imposed this burden on the Corinthians as Cephas (Peter, cf *Mark* 1:30) appears to have done, but it was to their benefit that he did not. 'The brethren of the Lord' is most naturally explained by supposing that they were the sons who were born to Joseph and Mary after the birth of Jesus [*Matt* 1:25; *John* 7:5; *Acts* 1:14; 1 *Cor* 15:7]. Paul specially mentions the name of Cephas 'as carrying weight with one partisan section at Corinth. "If your favourite leader does so, surely so may I"' (Fausset).

V6: Or I only and Barnabas, have we not a right to forbear working?

Paul's resolve to earn his own living by pursuing the trade he had learned in his youth was evidently shared by Barnabas, his companion on the first missionary journey, but apparently not by the other apostles. But instead of being grateful for his self-sacrifice the Corinthians thought that to engage in such manual labour was beneath the dignity of one who was truly an apostle [*Acts* 18:3, 20:34; 2 *Thess* 3:8]. Paul, however, here insists that his voluntary decision to support himself did not mean that he had renounced his right to be wholly maintained by those who benefited from his ministry.

V7: What soldier ever serveth at his own charges? who planteth a vineyard, and eateth not the fruit thereof? or who feedeth a flock, and eateth not of the milk of the flock?

The secular occupations Paul mentions to justify his right to maintenance as the equal of the other apostles are themselves types of the Christian ministry. 'The first represents the apostles going forth to wage war with the world; the second represents them, after conquest, planting churches; the third represents their pastoral care of the churches which they have founded. Again, the soldier is a mercenary; the vine-dresser an owner; the shepherd a slave. Yet in all alike labour implies reward' (Edwards). [*John* 21:15-17; 1 *Cor* 3:6, 7; 2 *Tim* 2:3-6]

V8: Do I speak these things after the manner of men? or saith not the law also the same?

But Paul does not rest his case on natural analogies alone, and his clinching argument is based upon the testimony of Scripture. He is not merely speaking 'after the manner of men', but is expounding the law of God. Although 'the law' is abolished as a means of obtaining salvation [*Rom* 3:19ff], it 'remains a revelation of truth and right [*Rom* 7:12ff], and Paul draws from it guidance for Christian conduct [cf 14:34; *Rom* 13:8ff]. The ethics of the New Testament are those of the Old, enhanced by Christ [see *Matt* 5:17ff]' (Findlay).

*V*9: **For it is written in the law of Moses, Thou shalt not muzzle the ox when he treadeth out the corn. Is it for the oxen that God careth,** 10: **or saith he it assuredly for our sake?**

'If God commands men to care for the oxen which tread out the corn, how much more does this principle hold good for ministers who labour to provide men with the Bread of Life?' [*Deut* 25:4; *Luke* 10:7; 1 *Tim* 5:18]. Calvin says that 'what Paul actually means is quite simple: though the Lord commands consideration for the oxen, he does so, not for the sake of the oxen, but rather out of regard for men, for whose benefit even the very oxen were created . . . You should understand, therefore, that God is not concerned about oxen, to the extent that oxen were the only creatures in his mind when he made the law, for he was thinking of men, and wanted to make them accustomed to being considerate in behaviour, so that they might not cheat the workman of his wages'.

*V*10b: **Yea, for our sake it was written: because he that ploweth ought to plow in hope, and he that thresheth,** *to thresh* **in hope of partaking.**

Yes, it was indeed written for our sake, because the ploughman ought to plough and the thresher to thresh in the hope of having a share of the crop. Thus the *principle* set forth in this command to care for the oxen is that the labourer shall partake of the fruit of his labour. 'The oxen cannot understand this even when they feed while threshing. It is said "altogether on our account", and it is a pity if we fail to understand' (Lenski).

*V*11: **If we sowed unto you spiritual things, is it a great matter if we shall reap your carnal things?**

It is here that Paul applies this principle to the work of the ministry, for this 'sowing' of spiritual things obviously refers to the preaching of the gospel. 'What they owed to him as their spiritual father admitted of no comparison with anything they could do for him in things temporal, though they might *express* it in the supply of his temporal wants' (David Brown).

*V*12: **If others partake of *this* right over you, do not we yet more? Nevertheless we did not use this right; but we bear all things, that we may cause no hindrance to the gospel of Christ.**

Paul does not blame the teachers who followed him in Corinth for exercising their right to receive support from the church, but simply points out that the founder of the church had even more right to it than they. But he never availed himself of this right, preferring to endure every kind of privation rather than hamper the progress of the gospel by leaving himself open to the charge of self-seeking.

*V*13: **Know ye not that they that minister about sacred things eat *of* the things of the temple, *and* they that wait upon the altar have their portion with the altar?**

Know ye not? Of course Paul's knowledgeable readers were familiar with the fact that those who served in the Temple in

Jerusalem received their living from the Temple; that those who waited on the altar were 'sharers in the altar' (Arndt-Gingrich). The terms Paul uses for 'temple' and 'altar' make it clear that he is not thinking of pagan worship, and he certainly would not have argued for the support of the Christian ministry from such idolatrous practices (cf 8:10 – 'the place of an idol' – Edwards). 'Paul argues by analogy from the Jewish priest to the Christian minister in respect of *the claim to maintenance;* we cannot infer from this *an identity of function*, any more than in the previous comparison with "the threshing ox"' (Findlay).

*V*14: **Even so did the Lord ordain that they that proclaim the gospel should live of the gospel.**

'As God enjoined under the law, so also Christ ordained in his church' (Edwards). In writing to Timothy Paul quotes *Luke* 10:7 [1 *Tim* 5:18]; here he gives its substance. Those who serve Christ in the ministry are to 'live *for* the gospel, and consequently ought also to live *of* the gospel. But woe to the man who claims to live *of* the gospel without living at the same time *for* the gospel!' (Godet).

*V*15: **But I have used none of these things: and I write not these things that it may be so done in my case; for** *it were* **good for me rather to die, than that any man should make my glorying void.**

Although Paul has proved the case for ministerial support, this implies no weakening of his own resolve to remain independent. He first states that he has used none of these privileges. The perfect tense 'affirms a settled position; the refusal has become a rule' (Findlay) [cf *v* 12]. Then Paul hastens to add that he is not writing these things from any ulterior motive. He is not making a subtle bid to secure such financial assistance from the Corinthians in the future. At this point the sentence is broken under the stress of his emotion (in the better attested text): **For I would rather die than—no, no one shall make this boast of mine an empty thing** (Barrett). 'He began to say that he *would rather die than be dependent* on Corinthian pay; he ends by saying, absolutely, he *will never be so dependent*' (Findlay).

*V*16: **For if I preach the gospel, I have nothing to glory of; for necessity is laid upon me; for woe is unto me, if I preach not the gospel.**

This introduces the reason for Paul's refusal to avail himself of these rights. Since he was conscripted into Christ's service against his previous will, he cannot glory in the fact that he preaches the gospel, for he preaches it from necessity rather than choice. A sovereignly determined commission gave him no ground for glorying in the service he was compelled to render. Hence he exclaims, 'Woe is unto me, if I preach not the gospel!' 'Had Paul disobeyed the call of God, his course from that time onwards must have been one of condemnation and misery. To fight against "Necessity" the Greeks conceived as ruin; their *necessity* was a blind, cruel Fate, Paul's *necessity* is the compulsion of Sovereign Grace' (Findlay).

*V*17: **For if I do this of mine own will, I have a reward: but if not of mine own will, I have a stewardship intrusted to me.**

Had Paul freely chosen to serve Christ, his voluntary labour would have merited a reward. But since he became an apostle under constraint, his position is merely that of a slave who has no part in choosing the stewardship which his master entrusts to him. What Paul means is that he can claim no credit for simply fulfilling the terms of his commission. Preach the gospel he *must*, but he *may* relinquish the pay which he feels a pressed man does not deserve; and so he chooses to receive another reward!

*V*18: **What then is my reward? That, when I preach the gospel, I may make the gospel without charge, so as not to use to the full my right in the gospel.**

Here we have Paul's paradoxical conclusion: his reward is found in refusing the reward! 'If he wished to exercise his privilege as an apostle for all that it was worth, he would insist upon full maintenance as his reward. But the reward which he prefers and gets is the delight of preaching without pay, of giving the Glad-tidings for nought, and taking no money for them' (Robertson – Plummer).

*V*19: **For though I was free from all *men*, I brought myself under bondage to all, that I might gain the more.**

Here the apostle begins to explain how he makes use of his freedom [*vv* 19-23]. In contrast to the proud inflexibility of his Corinthian critics, Paul's seemingly inconsistent behaviour is due to his ardent love for the souls of men. Free from all men, he has used this freedom to make himself the servant of all! Luther gave expression to the same paradox of grace when he said: 'A Christian man is a most free lord of all, subject to none. A Christian man is a most dutiful servant of all, subject to all'.

that I might gain the more. Paul is no universalist. He never did entertain the hope of winning 'the whole wide world for Jesus', nor did he pursue this course to gain more converts than any other apostle, but rather to win 'more than I should have gained if I had not made myself a slave to all' (Robertson – Plummer).

*V*20: **And to the Jews I became as a Jew, that I might gain Jews; to them that are under the law, as under**

the law, not being myself under the law, that I might gain them that are under the law;

Although Paul was no longer 'under the law', because he knew himself to be a new man in Christ [2 *Cor* 5:17], when he was among Jews he practised the customs he was not obliged to observe in order to gain them for Christ. But if he was always ready to respect Jewish scruples [*Acts* 16:3; 21:16], he was never prepared to sacrifice gospel principles to Jewish prejudice [*Gal* 2:5]. 'Paul is free from the ceremonial law through the work of Christ but he does not consider it a sin to observe the law, provided this was not done to acquire righteousness' (Grosheide). [cf *Rom* 10:3, 4; *Phil* 3:2ff]

V21: **to them that are without law, as without law, not being without law to God, but under law to Christ, that I might gain them that are without law.**

But when Paul was with Gentiles he dropped these Jewish customs which would have hindered his preaching the gospel to them. This did not mean, however, that he behaved as though he were under no law at all. On the contrary, all his actions were governed by the knowledge that he was 'subject to the law of Christ' (Arndt-Gingrich). Since Christ has changed Paul's relation to the law by fulfilling it on his behalf, he now recognizes the futility of that legalism which attempts to win salvation by its obedience to the law [*Rom* 10:4; *Gal* 3:13; *Phil* 3:9]. But because gospel freedom is not lawlessness, Paul also acknowledges his abiding obligation to obey the moral law [*Rom* 6:15, 13:8-10], and is enabled to live out its precepts through the mediation of his Redeemer [7:22, 23] and the power of the Spirit [*Rom* 8:4]. Grace does not therefore free the believer 'from the requirement of exact obedience, but from that rigour of obedience which the law required as a condition of salvation' (Samuel Bolton, *The True Bounds of Christian Freedom*, p. 40).

*V*22: **To the weak I became weak, that I might gain the weak: I am become all things to all men, that I may by all means save some.**

Paul next shows how the principle of accommodating himself to the needs of others applies to the actual situation in Corinth [8:13]. 'So well did he enter into the scruples of the timid and half-enlightened [e.g. 8:7, 10; *Rom* 14:1ff], that he forgot his own strength [8:4; *Rom* 15:1] and felt himself "weak" with them: cf 2 *Cor* 11:29, *who is weak, and I am not weak?*' (Findlay).

I am become all things to all men, that I may by all means save some. 'This does not mean that he will act in an unprincipled manner, or compromise on Christian principles; but he will sacrifice his own legitimate interests and preferences completely, if thereby he may save some' (Hillyer).

*V*23: **And I do all things for the gospel's sake, that I may be a joint partaker thereof.**

Unlike the selfish Corinthians, Paul does not equate the gospel with a false individualism. It is by devoting himself without reserve to the spiritual welfare of others that he ensures his own participation in the gospel. For though others may be saved through a work which is devoid of love, the preacher who lacks this love will not be saved. As Lenski remarks, Some preachers will think it strange that Paul would lose his own part in the gospel if he did not follow this one method of preaching the gospel [cf *v* 27], for they are sure that *they* will be saved no matter how they decide to preach it!

*V*24: **Know ye not that they that run in a race run all, but one receiveth the prize? Even so run; that ye may attain.**

V25: **And every man that striveth in the games exer-
ciseth self-control in all things. Now they *do it* to receive
a corruptible crown; but we an incorruptible.**

Paul selects a familiar figure to enforce the lesson of self-
discipline upon his readers, for the famous Isthmian Games
were held every two years in their neighbourhood. As
befits those who have entered a far sterner contest he exhorts
all to run as the one victor ran in the Greek games, though of
course this does not mean that in the Christian race only *one*
wins the prize.

It was well known that every athlete who entered for the
games had to undergo ten months' intensive training under
the direction of the judges, and was forced to adhere to a
strict diet [2 *Tim* 2:5]. In the same way the Christian athlete
must discipline himself to lay aside all that would hinder his
progress in the great race to gain the victor's crown ('every
weight' as well as every sin: *Heb* 12:1, 2). 'The pine crown
which the judge put on the victor's head in the Isthmian
Games, while it was the emblem of glory, was at the same
time the emblem of the transitory character of that glory.
For the spiritual victor there is reserved an unfading crown!'
(Godet). [2 *Tim* 4:8; 1 *Pet* 5:4]

V26: **I therefore so run, as not uncertainly; so fight I,
as not beating the air:**
V27: **but I buffet my body, and bring it into bondage:
lest by any means, after that I have preached to others,
I myself should be rejected.**

Here Paul lets the careless and self-indulgent Corinthians
know that he at least has entered the contest in earnest. He
does not run 'as one who has no fixed goal' (Arndt-Gingrich),
nor does he box as one who beats the air instead of his oppo-
nent, which in this case turns out to be his own body! How-

ever, in saying 'I give my body a black eye, and make it a slave' (Lenski), Paul is not providing a proof text for flagellants. He uses this language 'not because the body is necessarily evil, but because it is the weapon with which the law of sin and death fights us and, at the same time, the sphere within which the spiritual powers of evil come within our reach to be bruised and destroyed . . . The Christian victor does not destroy the body, but makes it his slave; so that it now serves the soul which it sought to slay' (Edwards). [*Rom* 6:12, 13]

lest by any means, after that I have preached to others, I myself should be rejected. (or 'disqualified' – Arndt-Gingrich) Paul seeks to awaken the Corinthians from their carnal slumbers by confronting them with this alarming thought. Be he even an inspired apostle, it is not enough to have preached to others if he fails to practise what he preaches. 'A preacher of salvation may yet miss it. He may show others the way to heaven, and never get thither himself . . . A holy fear of himself was necessary to preserve the fidelity of an apostle; and how much more necessary is it to our preservation? Note, Holy fear of ourselves, and not presumptuous confidence, is the best security against apostasy from God, and final rejection by him' (Matthew Henry).

CHAPTER TEN

The danger of believers presuming upon their spiritual privileges is illustrated by God's punishment of the Israelites for their idolatry, fornication, and murmuring. These things are written for our warning. But God will not permit his people to be tempted beyond their strength: there is always a way of escape [vv 1-13]. The Corinthians must flee from idolatry, for to participate in a sacrificial meal is to participate in worship, and they dare not provoke the Lord by holding communion with demons [vv 14-22]. But though they must shun idol-feasts, it is lawful to partake of idol-meats. Yet because love limits liberty, they are to abstain from eating such food in the presence of an over-scrupulous brother. In all things they must seek God's glory, and consult the good of others. This is Paul's own rule which he offers for their imitation [vv 23-11:1].

*V*1: **For I would not, brethren, have you ignorant, that our fathers were all under the cloud, and all passed through the sea;**

For I would not, brethren, have you ignorant, Paul does not wish them to overlook the importance of what he is about to say. 'This chapter is to be closely connected with 9:27. In the history of the chosen race we see men becoming *disqualified* and falling short of the promised inheritance.

But the warning is the more pointed inasmuch as the danger of the Corinthians and of the Israelites alike lay in contact with idolatry' (Edwards).

that our fathers The reason Paul uses this phrase in writing to Gentile 'brethren' is to emphasize the continuity of both dispensations [cf *Rom* 4.1, 11ff, 11:17f; *Gal* 3:7, 29; *Phil* 3:3]. 'The Jewish church is related as parent to the Christian church' (Fausset).

were all The example of Israel proves that the possession of great religious privileges does not guarantee immunity from divine judgment. The lesson is underscored by the solemn repetition of the word 'all' which is used five times in the first four verses. 'Those people who *almost all* perished, began with being *all* blessed of the Lord' (Godet).

under the cloud, i.e. under its guidance. 'The symbol of the divine presence and favour was before their eyes day and night. If any people ever had reason to think their salvation secure, it was those whom God thus wonderfully guided' (Hodge) [*Exod* 13:21, 22]

and all passed through the sea; 'Would God permit those to perish for whom he had wrought so signal a deliverance, and for whose sake he sacrificed the hosts of Egypt? Yet their carcasses were strewed in the wilderness'(Hodge).[*Numb*.14:29]

V2: **and were all baptized unto Moses in the cloud and in the sea;**

The Israelites 'had themselves baptized into Moses' (middle voice: expressing the voluntary nature of their act) when they crossed the Red Sea under his leadership [*Exod* 14:31]. Paul's argument is, 'The Corinthians, it is true, have been "baptized", but so also were the Israelites; if the virtual baptism of the latter availed not to save them from the doom of lust, neither will the actual baptism of the former save them' (Fausset).

As Paul appears to have coined this unique expression, 'baptized into Moses', to match his usual formula for baptism ('into Christ', cf *Rom* 6:3), the details of the description cannot be pressed. He simply means that the Israelites were surrounded by the cloud and the sea, though they were untouched by either. The point of the comparison both here and in 1 *Pet* 3:20f 'is not passing through the water but deliverance through a flood which separates the saved from the lost' (L. Goppelt, *TDNT*, Vol. 8, p. 331).

*V*3 : and did all eat the same spiritual food;

The Israelites were not only miraculously delivered from the Egyptian bondage, but they were also miraculously sustained in the wilderness by manna from heaven [*Ps* 78:24, 25]. This food not only nourished the body, but its supernatural origin ought also to have had the effect of constituting it 'spiritual food' for the soul. It is remarkable, observe Robertson and Plummer, that Paul 'chooses the manna and the rock, and not any of the Jewish sacrifices, as parallels to the Eucharist'.

*V*4 : and did all drink the same spiritual drink: for they drank of a spiritual rock that followed them: and the rock was Christ.

The manner in which the Israelites were supplied with water in the desert was no less miraculous [*Exod* 17:6; *Num* 20]. If Paul alludes here to the rabbinical legend that the rock from which the water gushed forth at Rephidim accompanied the Israelites on their journey, the word 'spiritual' clearly shows that he does so only to reject it; for as Findlay remarks, 'we must not disgrace Paul by making him say that the pre-incarnate Christ followed the march of Israel in the shape of a lump of rock!'

and the rock was Christ. Although they discerned it not, Christ himself was the author of all their blessings; an assertion which requires his pre-existence and tacitly assumes his Deity by giving him a title which was used of Jehovah in the Old Testament [*Deut* 32:15; *Ps* 18:2; *Is* 17:10, etc.]. The spiritual similarity of the two covenants, and of the gifts accompanying them, rests on this identity of the divine head of both. The practical consequence is obvious at a glance: Christ lived in the midst of the ancient people, and the people perished! How can you think yourselves, you Christians, secure from the same lot!' (Godet).

V5: **Howbeit with most of them God was not well pleased: for they were overthrown in the wilderness.**

A massive understatement, for of that first generation only Caleb and Joshua lived to enter the land of promise [*Heb* 3:17]. This does not mean, however, 'that all those who died in the wilderness were also forever damned. Some were saved although they suffered this temporal judgment because of their sins' (Lenski). [cf 11:30]

for they were overthrown in the wilderness. 'What a spectacle is that which is called up by the apostle before the eyes of the self-satisfied Corinthians: all those bodies, sated with miraculous food and drink, strewing the soil of the desert!' (Godet).

V6: **Now these things were our examples, to the intent we should not lust after evil things, as they also lusted.**

These judgments are not recorded in Scripture as matters of antiquarian interest which have no bearing on the contemporary scene in swinging first-century Corinth. On the contrary, they are beacons set to warn 'us' (all believers) *not* to follow Israel's example in lusting after evil things. The allusion is to their longing after the flesh-pots of Egypt, just as the appeal of good food might tempt the Corinthians to attend idolatrous banquets [*Num* 11:4-6]. Sin has its genesis in lust and Paul therefore places this first. Unless the first motions of sin's repulsive brood are remorselessly crushed they will *live* to bring forth *death*! [*Jas* 1:14, 15].

*V*7: **Neither be ye idolaters, as were some of them; as it is written, The people sat down to eat and drink, and rose up to play.**

The Corinthians must not fall into idolatry as the children of Israel did when they worshipped the golden calf. Paul aptly quotes *Exod* 32:6 because it would call to mind the feasting and licentious dancing which were associated with pagan worship in Corinth; for as the next verse shows, idolatry inevitably leads to immorality [cf *Rom* 1:24f].

*V*8: **Neither let us commit fornication, as some of them committed, and fell in one day three and twenty thousand.**

Paul here recalls the judgment which fell upon the Israelites when they committed fornication with the daughters of Moab at their idol-feasts [*Num* 25:1-9]. The warning was relevant in a city where the priestesses of the cult of Aphrodite were harlots! Paul gives the number slain as 23,000 whereas *Num* 25:9 has 24,000. But the difference is not important because both figures are obviously round numbers. It is therefore unreasonable to insist upon mathematical exactitude when the figures given are intended only to be approximate: 'more than 23,000 counted exactly, but not entirely 24,000. Taken in this sense, both figures are correct' (Lenski).

*V*9: **Neither let us make trial of the Lord, as some of them made trial and perished by the serpents.**

The Corinthians must not presume to put the Lord to the test as did the Israelites, for they complained that he had brought them into the desert to die and despised his provision for their needs. This daring experiment resulted in a punishment which made their complaint a dreadful reality, so that many of them 'lay a-perishing' where they had been bitten by the serpents [*Num* 21:4-9]. So Paul warns his readers not to try the Lord by resenting the restrictions of their new life in Christ. 'The Christian profession demanded that the Corinthians should forego the old heathen enjoyments. But instead of rejoicing in their deliverance through Christ the Corinthians were dissatisfied and longed for the old pagan celebrations' (Lenski).

*V*10: **Neither murmur ye, as some of them murmured, and perished by the destroyer.**

Another sin which called down the judgment of God upon the Israelites was their murmuring against his will as this was expressed through the mouth of his servants, Moses and Aaron [*Num* 16]. Let the Corinthians also beware of this sin, for such murmuring is the audible expression of distrust in God's guidance. 'Voices were begining to be raised against Paul among the Corinthians; if they remained unchecked, the gravest danger might result' (Lenski). As angels are often mentioned in Scripture as the agents of divine judgment, it is not surprising to find that Paul here refers the destruction of these rebels to the destroying angel of God [cf *Exod* 12:23].

*V*11: **Now these things happened unto them by way of example; and they were written for our admonition, upon whom the ends of the ages are come.**

Paul insists that these Old Testament incidents were recorded in Scripture with a view to the admonition of New Testament saints. It is because the judgments he cites were *exemplary* in their nature that they serve as a lesson for all time,

upon whom the ends of the ages are come. 'The New Testament dispensation winds up all former "ages". No new dispensation shall appear till Christ comes as Judge. The "ends" (plural) include various successive periods consummated and merging together [*Eph* 1:10: cf *Heb* 9:26]. Our dispensation being the consummation of all that went before, our responsibilities are the greater, and the greater our guilt, if we fall short of our privileges' (Fausset).

*V*12: **Wherefore let him that thinketh he standeth take heed lest he fall.**

In view of the foregoing examples the Corinthians must not presume that the mere possession of the privileges and gifts of the gospel can secure them against the possibility of falling from grace under all circumstances; that they did entertain such an illusory assurance is proved by their dangerously careless walk. 'Our security as it relates to God consists in faith; as it relates to ourselves, in fear' (Fausset).

*V*13: **There hath no temptation taken you but such as man can bear: but God is faithful, who will not suffer you to be tempted above that ye are able; but will with the temptation make also the way of escape, that ye may be able to endure it.**

But in case the Corinthians should fall a prey to despondency, Paul reminds them that so far they have not been assailed by such superhuman trials as would lead them to doubt God's ability to care for them in the future. They are to find comfort in the fact that God is faithful. This means he will not permit them to be tempted beyond their power; for with the temptation which he appoints, he also makes the way of escape so that they may be able to endure it. God thus tempers the length and strength of the temptation to enable his people to bear it and not be overwhelmed by it. Yet they would certainly 'fall' if they continued to court temptation by yielding to idolatry instead of using God's way of escape.

*V*14: **Wherefore, my beloved, flee from idolatry.**

Paul softens the tone but not the urgency of his admonition with the tender address 'my beloved'. He keeps up the metaphor of the previous verse, which is that of an army caught in a defile and urged to flee through the mountain pass (Edwards). They are not to stand and fight idolatry with their vaunted knowledge; their only safety is in flight. 'They must not try how near they can go, but how far they can fly' (Robertson – Plummer).

*V*15: **I speak as to wise men; judge ye what I say.**

Paul speaks without irony. He appeals to them as men with sufficient intelligence to judge the validity of the argument he is about to present to them. 'Ye' is emphatic: 'Do *ye* now judge it; *I* have done so' (Edwards).

*V*16: **The cup of blessing which we bless, is it not a communion of the blood of Christ? The bread which we break, is it not a communion of the body of Christ?**

Paul argues that if partaking of the Lord's Supper brings the Christian into communion with Christ, then it must follow that those who participate in idol-feasts are thereby brought into communion with demons [*vv* 16-22]. He mentions the cup first because he intends to enlarge upon the significance of eating sacrificial food [*v* 17f]. Paul does not call attention to the wine, but to the cup which makes it the symbol of Christ's death. It is only because Christ was willing to drain the cup of sin's bitter dregs that in his nail-pierced hands it becomes for us 'the cup of blessing' [*Luke* 22:20, 42]. Believers thus receive this cup from the Lord with thanksgiving, and 'we bless' shows that this 'consecration is the corporate act of the church' (Fausset).

The fact that Paul here refers to the sharing of the cup and the bread as a 'communion' of the blood and body of Christ proves that the Lord's Supper is something more than a memorial meal. For the believer shares in all the benefits of Christ's sacrifice as he partakes of the tokens by which it is recalled but not re-enacted. 'The bread and wine are vehicles of the presence of Christ. . . .Partaking of bread and wine is union (sharing) with the heavenly Christ' (E. Hauck, *TDNT*, Vol. 3, p. 805).

*V*17: **seeing that we, who are many, are one bread, one body: for we all partake of the one bread.**

Because there is one bread, we who are many are one body, for we all partake of the one bread. (RSV) This punctuation is to be preferred, for it is from the fact that there is but one bread, one Lord, one source of salvation, that Paul deduces the unity of the church. 'We are not said to be one bread; but we are one body because we partake of one bread. The design of the apostle is to show that every one who comes to the Lord's supper enters into communion with all other communicants. They form one body in virtue of their joint participation of Christ. This being the case, those who attend the sacrificial feasts of the heathen form one religious body. They are in religious communion with each other, because in communion with the demons on whom their worship terminates' (Hodge).

*V*18: **Behold Israel after the flesh: have not they that eat the sacrifices communion with the altar?**

Behold Israel after the flesh: The qualifying phrase 'after the flesh' brings out 'the external character of the Israelitish worship, in opposition to the spiritual worship of the true Israel, the church' (Godet).

have not they that eat the sacrifices communion with the altar?

The same principle held good in ancient Israel. To partake of the sacrifices brought the worshippers into communion with the altar, i.e. with all that it stood for. It is quite unnecessary to maintain that Paul is drawing a parallel between these Jewish sacrifices and the Lord's supper. J. B. Lightfoot decisively rejects the inference of some interpreters, that a comparison of 9:13 with this verse suggests that Paul 'recognizes the designation of the Lord's table as an altar. On the contrary it is a speaking fact, that in both passages he avoids using this term of the Lord's table, though the language of the context might readily have suggested it to him, if he had considered it appropriate. Nor does the argument in either case require or encourage such an inference' (*The Epistle to the Philippians*: 'Dissertation on the Christian Ministry', p. 266).

V19: What say I then? that a thing sacrificed to idols is anything, or that an idol is anything?

Paul pauses here to ask, 'Am I contradicting myself?' [cf 8:4]. Of course not! It is true that an idol lacks the reality attributed to it, and therefore what is offered to it in sacrifice is also devoid of any significance. So because this pagan rite can neither consecrate nor contaminate the food, believers may indeed buy and eat such meat without offence [vv 25, 27]. But to participate in heathen worship is a very different matter!

V20: But *I say*, that the things which the Gentiles sacrifice, they sacrifice to demons, and not to God:

and I would not that ye should have communion with demons.

Although the heathen divinities do not exist, it must not be supposed that idolatry is harmless, for it brings the worshipper into communion with demons! Paul's allusion to *Deut* 32:17 recalls Israel's departure from the law of God to sacrifice to demons; let not the Christians in Corinth fall into the same grave sin. The point is not what the worshipper intends, but what his worship actually effects.

*V*21: **Ye cannot drink the cup of the Lord, and the cup of demons: ye cannot partake of the table of the Lord, and of the table of demons.**

Ye cannot It is a *moral* impossibility for the Corinthians to partake of the Lord's table and of the table of demons. They must realize that these fellowships are mutually incompatible, since the kind of fellowship enjoyed by the guests is always determined by the character of the host at whose table they sit. If therefore they have accepted an engagement to sit at Christ's table, then they are no longer free to accept invitations to have communion with demons! Evidence has been found which shows that a pagan would hold such a meal for his friends in the idol's temple: 'Chairemon invites you to dinner at the table of the Lord Serapis in the Serapeum, tomorrow the 15th at the 9th hour' (*Papyrus Oxyrhynchus*, i. 110).

*V*22: **Or do we provoke the Lord to jealousy? are we stronger than he?**

Here Paul's language harks back to *Deut* 32:21, where the reference is to Israel's idolatry which provoked God's jealous anger. 'If the Corinthians *are* daring Christ's sovereign displeasure by coquetting with idolatry, they must suppose themselves "stronger than he"! As sensible and prudent men they must see the absurdity, as well as the awful peril, of such double-dealing' (Findlay).

*V*23 : **All things are lawful; but not all things are expedient. All things are lawful; but not all things edify.**

Here Paul, returning to the principle of Christian licence in things indifferent, first repeats the slogan of the libertines with the same answer he gave to it in 6:12, but with his second quotation of 'All things are lawful' he returns to the note which was struck in 8:1. He insists that the Christian may not assert his 'rights' to the spiritual detriment of his fellow-believers, but must at all times use his freedom to build up the body to which he belongs. 'A liberty which harms others is not likely to benefit oneself, and a liberty which harms oneself is not likely to benefit others. Cf 14:26; *Rom* 14:19' (Robertson – Plummer).

*V*24 : **Let no man seek his own, but** *each* **his neighbour's good.**

A succinct statement of the principle by which Christian conduct is to be regulated! Self-seeking love must give place to self-giving love [cf *Rom* 15:2; *Phil* 2:4]. In applying this rule to the question under discussion, 'two cases might present themselves to the Christian: that of a meal in his own house [*vv* 25, 26], or that of a meal in a strange house [*vv* 27-30]' (Godet).

*V*25 : **Whatsoever is sold in the shambles, eat, asking no question for conscience' sake;** *v* 26. **for the earth is the Lord's, and the fulness thereof.**

The 'shambles' was the food market which included the meat market, and in Corinth as in Pompeii, most of the meat sold there would come from the beasts which were sacrificed in the temple that was situated nearby. Paul sides with the strong in affirming that whatever is offered for sale in the market may be eaten 'without raising any question on the ground of conscience' (RSV). Incidentally, this counsel reflects Paul's own emancipation from all Jewish food laws [cf 1 *Tim* 4:3-5], though among Jews he conformed to their ways to avoid giving needless offence [9:20]. That this is the right attitude towards food is confirmed by his appeal to *Ps* 24:1, which was used by the Jews as a 'grace before meat', and perhaps its quotation here already points to the Christian adoption of this practice.

*V*27: **If one of them that believe not biddeth you** *to a feast*, **and ye are disposed to go; whatsoever is set before you, eat, asking no question for conscience' sake.**

A Christian is also free to accept an invitation to share a meal with an unbeliever in his home. 'As the sacrifices lost their religious character when sold in the market, so also at any private table they were to be regarded not as sacrifices, but as ordinary food, and might be eaten without scruple. The apostle did not prohibit the Christians from social intercourse with the heathen. If invited to their tables, they were at liberty to go' (Hodge).

*V*28: **But if any man say unto you, This hath been offered in sacrifice, eat not, for his sake that showed it, and for conscience' sake:** *v* 29a: **conscience, I say, not thine own, but the other's;**

But if someone, presumably a fellow-believer with an overscrupulous conscience, should say that the food provided at the meal had been offered in sacrifice, then it must be refused in conformity with the principle laid down in *v* 24. It is precisely because his conscience *is* weak that he still calls it 'sacrificial food' rather than 'idol-meat', for to him there is still something 'sacred' about it. He is not yet free of the old heathen superstitions. And so though the strong believer knows that he is free to eat it, he must abstain out of respect for his weaker brother's scruples.

*V*29b: **for why is my liberty judged by another's conscience?**
*V*30: **If I partake with thankfulness, why am I evil spoken of for that for which I give thanks?**

This does not mean that the strong Christian is called upon to forfeit his inner conviction concerning the lawfulness of eating such food, but he is voluntarily to restrict his use of this liberty of conscience in the interest of the weaker conscience of his brother. Thus in *principle* Paul is free to eat anything, for he has not surrendered his liberty at the behest of another's conscience; but in *practice* he avoids having his liberty denounced by refusing to exercise it in the presence of the weak. The very fact that he can give thanks for his food proves that he eats it with a clear conscience, but he will not allow that for which he gives thanks to wound the conscience of his weaker brethren.

*V*31: **Whether therefore ye eat, or drink, or whatsoever ye do, do all to the glory of God.**

The whole discussion is now summed up in this comprehensive principle. Christians are not to consult their own inclinations, but in all their actions the paramount consideration must be the glory of God. It is only when this thought motivates the conduct of men that the best interests of others can be secured. For the showing of love to our neighbour is the corollary of our love to God.

*V*32: **Give no occasion of stumbling, either to Jews, or to Greeks, or to the church of God:**

'Some may, indeed, *take* offence, namely, wrongfully; we

are not to *give* offence. The former no Christian can avoid; the latter all Christians are to avoid' (Lenski). Paul speaks of three categories of existence: Jews, Greeks, and Christians, who are neither Jewish nor Gentile; for the church of God is a new society whose members form a 'new race' (so F. F. Bruce).

*V*33: **even as I also please all men in all things, not seeking mine own profit, but the *profit* of the many, that they may be saved.**

Unlike the spiritually immature Corinthians Paul does not live for his own advantage, but for the benefit of the many. He seeks not to please himself, but to please all men in all things in order that they may be saved [9:22]. Of course he could not attain such a holy end by 'pleasing' men in sinful ways. He could never sacrifice principle [*Gal* 2:5], descend to dissimulation [*Gal* 2:13, 14], or compromise the truth [*Acts* 20:27], in the interests of gaining more souls for Christ!

Ch 11. *V* 1: **Be ye imitators of me, even as I also am of Christ.**

Although Paul did not know Christ after the flesh [2 *Cor* 5:16], it would be quite wrong to suggest that he took no interest in the earthly life of Jesus. In *Rom* 15:2f he directly proposes the example of Christ for the imitation of his readers, and here he urges his own example insofar as he follows that of Christ. 'It is a very important trait, that Paul feels himself to be an imitator of Christ in his practical conduct. He could not say and be this, unless he had a living concrete picture of the ethical personality of Jesus' (J. Weiss).

CHAPTER ELEVEN

Paul next corrects disorders in the worship of the church. He deals first with the decorum and dress of women. It appears that in their new-found freedom they had put off the veil which was then the recognized symbol of their subordination to man. But he insists that equality in grace does not set aside the requirements of the social order which even nature teaches us to respect [vv 2-16]. Secondly, he rebukes them for their disgraceful abuse of the Lord's Supper. This divine ordinance was profaned by their dissension, excesses, and selfishness. To rectify these disorders which had brought grievous judgments upon the church, he reminds them of the nature and purpose of this sacred meal, and warns against the partaking of it unworthily [vv 17-34].

*V*1: has been placed at the end of the previous chapter where it properly belongs.

*V*2: **Now I praise you that ye remember me in all things, and hold fast the traditions, even as I delivered them to you.**

This new section of the Epistle is prefaced with a word of praise, though this is later balanced with a word of rebuke [*v* 17]. Paul gladly acknowledges that in general the congregation at Corinth remains obedient to the precepts which he had handed down to them. The early church received the oral tradition of the apostles with the same respect that she was to accord to their written testimony, because she recognized in both the voice of her risen and exalted Lord [11:23, 15:2; 2 *Thess* 2:15]. 'We shall search in vain for any suggestion that one possesses a greater measure of inspiration than the other. The one and only source of the teaching was Christ; from him the stream flows, Scripture and "tradition" are blended in one great luminous river of truth, and do not separate into divergent streams till later times. They were at first two forms of the same thing. Both together constitute the Tradition, the Canon or Rule of Faith' (J. F. Bethune-Baker cited by N. Geldenhuys, *Supreme Authority*, p. 116).

V3: **But I would have you know, that the head of every man is Christ; and the head of the woman is the man; and the head of Christ is God.**

But Paul wishes the Corinthians to know that though all men are not members of the body of which Christ is the head, every man whether he knows it or not is nevertheless subject to the *headship* or government of Christ. In a less absolute sense every woman is by order of creation under the headship of man, and the equality of the sexes in the realm of grace does not abolish this distinction between them when they become subject to church order and discipline. The Christian women of Corinth will find this truth easier to accept if they remember that as Mediator even Christ himself is subject to God. 'God is the Head of Christ, not in respect of his essence and divine nature, but in respect of his office as Mediator; as the man is the head of the woman, not in respect of a different and more excellent essence and nature, (for they are both of the same nature,) but in respect of office and place, as God hath set him over the woman' (Poole).

*V*4: **Every man praying or prophesying, having his head covered dishonoureth his head.**

It is not likely that men were actually covering their heads for worship in Corinth. Paul puts the case hypothetically to complete his argument [*v* 5]. It is important to note that he first uses 'head' in the literal sense, and then metaphorically of Christ's headship [*v* 3]. 'The man that shames his natural head shames also his spiritual head; that is, he that shames himself by wearing a symbol of subjection to the woman, shames Christ, to whom alone God has subjected him' (Edwards).

*V*5: **But every woman praying or prophesying with her head unveiled dishonoureth her head; for it is one and the same thing as if she were shaven.**

This verse does not necessarily sanction women speaking in church, 'even though possessing miraculous gifts; but simply records what took place at Corinth, reserving the censure till 14:34, 35. Even those "prophesying" women were to exercise their gift rather in other times and places than the public congregation' (Fausset). [*Acts* 2:18; 21:9]

for it is one and the same thing as if she were shaven. In Greece only immoral women, so numerous in Corinth, went about unveiled; slave-women wore the shaven head which was also a punishment of the adulteress; 'with these the Christian woman who emancipates herself from becoming restraints of dress, is in effect identified. To shave the head is to carry out thoroughly its unveiling, to remove nature's as well as fashion's covering [*v* 15]' (Findlay).

*V*6: **For if a woman is not veiled, let her also be shorn: but if it is a shame to a woman to be shorn or shaven, let her be veiled.**

These imperatives are not to be understood literally; they only show what consistency requires. Let the woman who discards the veil take her defiance of modesty to its logical conclusion. 'If a woman prefers a bare head, she should remove her hair; womanly feeling forbids the latter, then it should forbid the former, for the like shame attaches to both' (Findlay).

*V*7: **For a man indeed ought not to have his head veiled, forasmuch as he is the image and glory of God: but the woman is the glory of the man.**

Although *Gen* 1:27 clearly states that God's image in 'man' includes both sexes, the fact that woman mediately derives her being from man means that she only partakes in the image of God through him [*vv* 8, 9]. Hence Paul does not here add that woman is the 'image' of man; she is not man's reflection, but his counterpart. 'It follows that he who degrades a woman sullies his manhood, and is the worst enemy of his race; the respect shown to women is the measure and safeguard of human dignity' (Findlay).

*V*8: **For the man is not of the woman; but the woman of the man:** *v* 9: **for neither was the man created for the woman; but the woman for the man:**

Paul insists that the facts of creation cannot be reversed or set aside. Man did not take his origin from woman, but woman from man [*Gen* 2:21–23]; he was not created for her, but she for him [*Gen* 2:18]. Scripture thus confronts the militant supporters of Women's Lib with 'the fact that the origin and *raison d'être* of woman are to be found in man' (H. Schlier, *TDNT*, Vol. III, p. 679).

*V*10: **for this cause ought the woman to have *a sign of authority* on her head, because of the angels.**

Since woman's subjection to man is a divine appointment, she is to cover her head in recognition of the place assigned to her in the created order, and this *veiling* is the *sign* of her 'authority' to approach God in public worship. Paul adds that this is to be done 'because of the angels'. As God's good angels are present when Christians meet together for worship great care must be taken not to offend them by any impropriety [cf 4:9; *Heb* 1:14]. Such an offence would occur if women discarded the veil and thereby displayed their disregard for the station given to them by their creation.

*V*11: **Nevertheless, neither is the woman without the man, nor the man without the woman, in the Lord.** *V*12: **For as the woman is of the man, so is the man also by the woman; but all things are of God.**

But though man has been given the superior place, this gives him no right to regard woman as an inferior being, for the sexes are inter-dependent and neither is complete without the other. The phrase 'in the Lord' points to the sphere where woman's rights are realized as nowhere in heathenism [cf *Gal* 3:28; *Eph* 5:28]. 'As woman was formed *out of* man, even so is man born *by means of* woman; but all things (including both man and woman) are *from* God as their source [*Rom* 11:36; 2 *Cor* 5:18]. They depend each on the other, and both on Him' (Fausset).

*V*13: **Judge ye in yourselves: is it seemly that a woman pray unto God unveiled?**

'This is an appeal to their own sense of propriety. The apostle often recognizes the intuitive judgments of the mind as authoritative [*Rom* 1:32, 3:8]. The constitution of our nature being derived from God, the laws which he has impressed upon it are as much a revelation from him as any other possible communication of his will. And to deny this, is to deny the possibility of all knowledge' (Hodge).

*V*14: **Doth not even nature itself teach you, that, if a man have long hair, it is a dishonour to him?**
*V*15: **But if a woman have long hair, it is a glory to her: for her hair is given her for a covering.**

'Nature' here means 'a sense of what is seemly springing from a real distinction in the constitution of things' (Edwards). Natural sentiment is reflected by universal custom. Long hair is felt to be a 'dishonour' to man because it is a contradiction of his manliness, whereas it is the glory of a woman: 'what is discreditable in the one is delightful in the other' (Findlay). Thus what has been given to woman as a natural covering ought to teach her the propriety of donning the veil in worship.

*V*16: **But if any man seemeth to be contentious, we have no such custom, neither the churches of God.**

Paul refuses to discuss the matter further with the man who is so contentious as to dispute his conclusion. 'If, after all that the apostle has advanced in maintenance of the modest distinction between the sexes, any one is still minded to debate, he must be put down by *authority* – that of Paul himself and his colleagues, supported by universal Christendom; cf 14:33, 37ff' (Findlay).

*V*17: **But in giving you this charge, I praise you not, that ye come together not for the better but for the worse.**

'This charge' is more likely to refer to the preceding injunction than to what follows. Paul cannot praise them for allowing the women to worship with unveiled heads, but the disorder with which he is about to deal is far more serious, for it means that they 'come together not for the better but for the worse'. 'That is, your public assemblies are so conducted that evil rather than good results. The censure is general, embracing all the grounds of complaint which are specified in this and the following chapters' (Hodge).

*V*18: **For first of all, when ye come together in the church, I hear that divisions exist among you; and I partly believe it.**

Here Paul begins to press charges against the Corinthians, but though his indictment extends as far as 14:40 there is no 'secondly' forthcoming. He has heard from a reliable but unnamed source that when the church meets together for worship there are 'divisions' among the members. Its *outward* congregational unity is marred by the unhappy *inward* divisions which separate clique from clique. The apostle seems to be referring to social discrimination rather than to party-spirit, as in 1:10. For in *v* 22 the rich are rebuked for refusing to share their food with the poorer members of the church. Paul is reluctant to believe all he has heard to their disadvantage in this matter, but what he is forced to believe is enough to earn his sternest censure. 'There may be schism, where there is no separation of communion. Persons may come together in the same church, and sit down at the same table of the Lord, and yet be schismatics. Uncharitableness, alienation of affection, especially if it grows up to discord, and feuds, and contentions, constitute schism' (Matthew Henry).

*V*19: **For there must be also factions among you, that they that are approved may be made manifest among you.**

'To the simple divisions which arise from personal preferences or aversions, Paul foresees that there will succeed divisions

of a far more profound nature, founded on opposite con-
ceptions of Christian truth. He believes what is told him of
the first, because he even expects the second. There will arise
among them false doctrines, *heresies*, according to the meaning
which the Greek term has taken in later ecclesiastical language,
and thence will follow much graver disruptions than the
present divisions. . . The Second Epistle to the Corinthians
shows in how brief a period this anticipation of the apostle
was realized' (Godet). [cf *Matt* 18:7; *Acts* 20:29, 30]

**that they that are approved may be made manifest
among you.**

Nevertheless there is a divine purpose fulfilled in these
heresies which 'are a magnet attracting unsound and unsettled
minds, and leaving genuine believers to stand out "approved"
by their constancy' (Findlay). Thus those who are approved of
God are made known to men [2 *Thess* 2:11, 12].

*V*20: **When therefore ye assemble yourselves together,
it is not possible to eat the Lord's supper:**

This sets forth the precise nature of the apostle's censure.
'The disorders at Corinth are so serious that when the church
meets for the sacrament it is not *the Lord's* supper that is eaten.
The disorders have given it a different character. It is no
longer *the Lord's*' (Morris).

*V*21: **for in your eating each one taketh before *other* his
own supper; and one is hungry, and another is drunken.**

The loveless abuse of the Love-feast (Agape) in Corinth was a
blatant denial of the fellowship which this common meal was
intended to express, for when each selfishly ate his own supper
it became morally impossible to eat the Lord's supper. 'Of all
imaginable schisms the most shocking: hunger and intoxi-

cation side by side, at what is supposed to be the Table of the Lord! This is indeed "meeting for the worse"' (Findlay).

*V*22: **What, have ye not houses to eat and to drink in? or despise ye the church of God, and put them to shame that have not? What shall I say to you? shall I praise you? In this I praise you not.**

Paul now ironically enquires whether such surfeiting means that the rich have no homes in which to eat and drink, or is it rather that in shaming the poor in this way they are showing their contempt for the congregation *of God*? [*James* 1:9, 10; 2:2–9]. Can he praise them for such conduct? 'In this I praise you not!' His restrained response is heavy with blame.

*V*23a: **For I received of the Lord that which also I delivered unto you,**

For the tradition which I handed on to you came to me from the Lord himself: (NEB) 'Paul means by this tradition, without doubt, the message that he had received from the original witnesses. Nevertheless he writes that he has for himself (i.e., as apostle) received the deliverances "from the Lord". He means specifically the ascended Lord. The testimony of the eyewitnesses is for him as apostle the delivered word of the glorified Lord. And as such he himself delivers it to the church of Corinth' (H. Ridderbos, 'The Canon of the New Testament' in *Revelation and the Bible*, p. 194). Oscar Cullmann also points out that the words 'from the Lord' can 'quite well mean a direct communication from the Lord, without it being necessary to think of a vision or to exclude intermediaries through whom the Lord himself transmits the "tradition". . .(for) it is the united testimony of all the apostles which constitutes the Christian "tradition", in which the "Lord" himself is at work' (*The Early Church*, p. 68). [1 *Cor* 15:11; *Gal* 1:16]

*V*23b: **that the Lord Jesus in the night in which he was betrayed took bread;** *v* 24: **and when he had given thanks, he brake it, and said, This is my body, which is for you: this do in remembrance of me.** *v* 25: **In like manner also the cup, after supper, saying, This cup is the new covenant in my blood: this do, as often as ye drink** *it***, in remembrance of me.**

Paul begins his account of the Lord's Supper by reminding the thoughtless Corinthians of the poignant fact that Jesus appointed it on the very night of his betrayal by Judas [cf *Matt* 26:26f; *Mark* 14:22f; *Luke* 22:17f]. After the Lord had offered a prayer of thanksgiving for the bread, he broke it in token of his bruised and broken body [*Is* 53:5]. 'The *breaking* of the bread involves its *distribution*, and reproves the Corinthians at the love feast: "every one taketh before other his own supper"' (Fausset).

This is my body, which is for you: The visible presence of Jesus made it impossible for those who were present at the institution of the Supper literally to identify the bread with his body. 'Jesus takes the bread which is before him, and presenting it to his disciples, he gives it to them as the *symbol* of his body which is about to be given up for them on the cross, and to become the means of their salvation; the verb *be* is taken in the same sense as that in which we say, as we look at a portrait: it *is* so and so!' (Godet).

this do in remembrance of me. As the celebration of the Passover vividly recalled Israel's historic redemption from the land of bondage, so Christians are bidden to keep on doing this as the means of bringing before their minds the price once paid by Christ to ransom them from their slavery to sin [cf 5:7]. 'The words of Christ contain two distinct but connected ideas. The one implies His presence in the sacrament:

[163]

"this is my body; this is my blood." The other implies His absence: "in remembrance of me." Both meet in the apostle's word, "communion" [cf 10:16], which involves, first, that the communicant appropriates Christ, and, second, that the instrument of this appropriation is conscious, voluntary faith. Appropriation of Christ necessitates His real presence; faith implies His equally real absence' (Edwards).

This cup is the new covenant in my blood: The word 'covenant' points to a unilateral disposition made by God in favour of man, and is not to be understood in terms of a mutual agreement made between two parties of equal standing. Christ made the Mosaic covenant 'old' when he referred to his death as the fulfilment of Jeremiah's prophecy of the 'new covenant' [*Jer* 31:31–34]. The shedding of blood was the basis upon which the distinctive blessings promised under both covenants were bestowed, but the first covenant became 'old' because it rested upon the repeated offering of typical sacrifices which could never take away sins, whereas the second remains 'new' because its gracious provisions have been forever secured by Christ's one real and final atonement for the sins of his people [*Heb* 9:18–10:14].

this do, as often as ye drink *it*, **in remembrance of me.** 'The Lord's supper brings to our *remembrance* Christ's sacrifice once-for-all for the full and final *remission of sins*. Not "do this for a *memorial* of me", as if it were a *memorial sacrifice* . . . a *reminding* the Father of his Son's sacrifice. Nay, it is for our *remembrance* of it, not to *remind* him' (Fausset).

*V*26: **For as often as ye eat this bread, and drink the cup, ye proclaim the Lord's death till he come.**

This begins Paul's own exposition of the significance of the Supper. In reminding the Corinthians of the solemnity of the occasion it recalls, he rebukes them for the irreverent manner in which they met together to celebrate it. 'The pathos and glory of the Table of the Lord were alike lost on the Corinthians' (Findlay).

For as often as ye eat this bread, and drink the cup, As J. Behm points out, Paul never speaks of eating the body or drinking the blood of Christ, but rather points to the repetition of the whole act by which believers are united with their Lord in intimate table fellowship, so that they participate in the fruit of his work on their behalf. 'The wholly realistic but spiritual and historical understanding of the Lord's Supper which we find in Paul is equally distinct both from a spiritualising which makes the sacrament a mere symbol and from a materialising which sanctifies things and deifies nature' (*TDNT*, Vol. III, p. 740).

ye proclaim the Lord's death till he come. Paul places the emphasis on the words by which the Lord's death is proclaimed in the Supper, and shows that this testimony to his finished work is to continue 'till he come'. The sacrament therefore not only recalls what was achieved by Christ's death but also looks forward to his return in glory. 'The church crying **Maranatha** testifies to the living, victorious Lord; it not only waits on him but waits for him' (Moffatt). [Cf 16:22].

*V*27: **Wherefore whosoever shall eat the bread or drink the cup of the Lord in an unworthy manner, shall be guilty of the body and the blood of the Lord.**

Paul solemnly warns the Corinthians that whoever treats the Supper of the Lord as his own supper profanes this means of grace and puts himself alongside those who crucified Christ [*vv* 21, 29]. The verse condemns the Romish practice of withholding the cup from the laity. 'How could anyone be guilty of drinking the cup of the Lord in an unworthy manner if the cup were not given to him? This is clearly one more instance in which the Church of Rome has taken it upon herself to alter the commands of the gospel' (L. Boettner, *Roman Catholicism*, p. 236).

*V*28: **But let a man prove himself, and so let him eat of the bread, and drink of the cup.**
*V*29: **For he that eateth and drinketh, eateth and drinketh judgment unto himself, if he discern not the body.**

Paul says 'Let a man test himself'. This means he must not come to this table in a spirit which is unworthy of it. Let him come with love towards his fellow-believers, so that he can do this in remembrance of the Lord. Such self-examination is necessary because the man who fails to discern the sacred character of this meal, so far from furthering his salvation actually eats and drinks to his own condemnation (not 'damnation' as in AV). Paul refers to the Lord's '*once for all sacrificed body*, discerned by the soul in faithful receiving; not present in the elements themselves' (Fausset). [*Acts* 3:21]

*V*30: **For this cause many among you are weak and sickly, and not a few sleep.**

Paul traces the prevalence of sickness and death among the Corinthians to this failure to discern 'the body', and thus warns them against continuing to profane the Lord's table. 'The mortality at Corinth began at God's house, and that for unworthy communicating. God will be sanctified of all that draw near to him. He loves to be acquainted with men in the walks of their obedience, and yet he takes state upon him in his ordinances, and will be served like himself, or we shall hear from him. What manner of men therefore ought we to be that come so near to God in this holy ordinance?' (Trapp). [1 *Pet* 4:17]

*V*31: **But if we discerned ourselves, we should not be judged.**
*V*32: **But when we are judged, we are chastened of the Lord, that we may not be condemned with the world.**

If the Corinthians would but examine themselves, so that they came to the Lord's Supper in the right spirit, they would not incur these disciplinary judgments [cf 5:5]. For though they are judged for their sinful conduct, yet this is done in order that they should not have to undergo the sharp verdict of *condemnation* with the world in the last judgment.

*V*33: **Wherefore, my brethren, when ye come together to eat, wait one for another. *V* 34: If any man is hungry, let him eat at home; that your coming together be not unto judgment. And the rest will I set in order whensoever I come.**

In conclusion Paul appeals to his brethren not to fracture their fellowship by each going 'ahead with his own meal' [*v* 21], but to wait for one another. And if any man is too hungry to wait for the others, he should satisfy his appetite at home. Such love feasts 'were not meals to satiate the bodily appetites, but were for a higher and holier purpose: let the hungry take off the edge of his hunger at home: see *v* 22' (Alford).

And the rest will I set in order whensoever I come. Matters of less pressing importance concerning the administration of the Lord's Supper could be left until Paul's next visit to Corinth whenever that might be. Since no one can possibly know what things he then intended to set in order it is in vain that Rome appeals to this text to justify her unwritten 'apostolic' traditions! 'If the fixing of the canon (of Scripture) had been carried out by the Church on the tacit assumption that its teaching-office, that is, the *subsequent* traditions, should be set alongside this canon with an *equal normative authority*, the reason for the creation of the canon would be unintelligible' (Oscar Cullmann, *The Early Church*, p. 92).

CHAPTER TWELVE

On the question of spiritual gifts Paul lays down the principle that only those which glorify Christ are of divine origin [vv 1–3]. It is the Holy Spirit who assigns the various gifts of wisdom, knowledge, faith, and tongues to each member for the good of the whole body to which he belongs [vv 4–11]. For in the church as in the human body, every member is useful and necessary, and so none is to be despised. The Corinthians are to recognize that God has set the individual members in their places to form one body as it pleased him. And since this unity involves mutual dependence it must promote mutual love [vv 12–26]. Clearly not all are apostles, teachers, and speakers in tongues, for God's gifts are distributed as he pleases; yet they should earnestly desire his best gifts for use in his service [vv 27–31].

V1: Now concerning spiritual *gifts*, brethren, I would not have you ignorant.

The words suggest that Paul's discussion of the miraculous or charismatic gifts of the Spirit is in response to a question put to him by the Corinthians [cf 7:1]. He wishes them to understand the common origin and aim of these supernatural endowments, so that they would be able to distinguish between the true and false claimants to the possession of them.

*V*2: **Ye know that when ye were Gentiles *ye were* led away unto those dumb idols, howsoever ye might be led.**

Paul here recognizes that religious ecstasy is not a distinctively Christian phenomenon. It is because heathenism also has its ecstatics that a criterion is necessary to prevent the Corinthians in their enthusiasm for these extraordinary manifestations from receiving every ecstatic utterance as the work of the Spirit [cf the later warning of 1 *John* 4:1–3]. Paul says in effect: 'In your pagan days you were helplessly led astray. In your devotion to dumb idols you experienced a form of demonic frenzy which carried you away, for then you had no fixed principle to guide you!' [cf 10:19ff].

*V*3: **Wherefore I make known unto you, that no man speaking in the Spirit of God saith, Jesus is anathema; and no man can say, Jesus is Lord, but in the Holy Spirit.**

Paul thus wishes the Corinthians to grasp the fact that not every form of religious ecstasy is inspired by the Holy Spirit, for no man who is speaking under his influence could possibly say, 'ANATHEMA JESUS', i.e. 'Jesus is accursed!' It would appear that a member of the congregation in Corinth had been guilty of giving utterance to this blasphemy under the mistaken impression that he was making a contribution to the worship of the church. But since God has already made Jesus LORD, and the Holy Spirit has been given specifically to glorify Jesus as LORD, it is evident that *He* cannot move men to say anything which detracts in the least degree from this DIVINE LORDSHIP [*Rom* 10:9]. On the contrary, it is only through the gracious ministry of the Spirit that any man can say that 'Jesus is LORD', for such supernatural confession of faith requires nothing less than a supernatural revelation of its truth [*Matt* 16:16, 17].

"In stating this first negative criterion, the apostle therefore means to say to the Corinthians: However ecstatic in form, or profound in matter, may be a spiritual manifestation, tongue, prophecy, or doctrine, if it tends to degrade Jesus, to make him an imposter or a man worthy of the divine wrath, if it does violence in any way to his holiness, you may be sure the inspiring breath of such a discourse is not that of God's Spirit' (Godet).

V4: **Now there are diversities of gifts, but the same Spirit.**
V5: **And there are diversities of ministrations, and the same Lord.**
V6: **And there are diversities of workings, but the same God, who worketh all things in all.**

There are distributions of gifts, but the same Spirit; there are distributions of services, and the same Lord; and there are distributions of operations, but the same God who operates all things in all men (Barrett). Paul next corrects the Corinthians for failing to discern the divine unity of purpose in the distribution of spiritual gifts among them. This differentiation had caused rivalry and division in the church, but boasting and jealousy are alike excluded by the realization that the disposition of these gifts is made in accordance with the sovereign will of the Triune God [*v* 11]. 'Uniformity of experience and service is not to be expected; unity lies ultimately in the Spirit who gives, the Lord who is served, the God who is at work – the Trinitarian formula is the more impressive because it seems to be artless and unconscious. Paul found it natural to think and write in these terms' (Barrett). [2 *Cor* 13:14; *Eph* 4:4–6]

V7: **But to each one is given the manifestation of the Spirit to profit withal.**

To each is given the manifestation of the Spirit for the common good (RSV). Moreover, in the communication to each of a particular gift the Spirit manifests himself for the benefit of all believers. 'When, therefore, the gifts of God, natural or supernatural, are perverted as a means of self-exaltation or aggrandizement it is a sin against their giver, as well as against those for whose benefit they were intended' (Hodge).

*V*8: **For to one is given through the Spirit the word of wisdom; and to another the word of knowledge, according to the same Spirit:** *v*9: **to another faith, in the same Spirit; and to another gifts of healings, in the one Spirit;** *v*10: **and to another workings of miracles; and to another prophecy; and to another discernings of spirits: to another *divers* kinds of tongues; and to another the interpretation of tongues:**

All the gifts listed here were supernatural endowments of the Spirit which were as temporary in their manifestation as was the apostolic office itself; 'the extraordinary gifts belonged to the extraordinary office and showed themselves only in connection with its activities' (B. B. Warfield, 'The Cessation of the Charismata', *Counterfeit Miracles*, p. 23). Hence it is hardly surprising that today we are unable exactly to determine the nature of these gifts and how they were exercised in the apostolic church. Paul begins with the highest of these gifts and proceeds to the least useful of them. Findlay makes the following helpful classification, using 1 *Cor* 14:14–20 as the basis of this discrimination:

I. Gifts which exhibit the Spirit working *through the* mind: The word of wisdom and the word of knowledge.

II. Gifts which exhibit the Spirit working *in distinction from the* mind: Faith, Healing, Miracles, Prophecy, and Discerning of spirits.

III. Gifts which exhibit the Spirit working *in supersession of the* mind: Tongues and their interpretation (the omission of these from the lists of gifts in *Rom* 12:3–8 and *Eph* 4:7–11 is significant and should not be overlooked).

1–2. the utterance of wisdom and **the utterance of knowledge** (RSV).
According to James Dunn, Paul here rebukes Corinthian pride in 'wisdom' and 'knowledge' by confining the gift to the *actual utterance* which reveals some aspect of wisdom and knowledge, and so serves to build up the community (*Jesus and the Spirit*, p 221). Since these gifts are placed first, a comparison with *v* 28 would seem to suggest that they both belonged to the apostolic office; and if the first characterized their inspired proclamation of the gospel [cf ch 1–2], the second would presumably describe their rôle as the inspired teachers of the church.

3. faith This is not saving faith, for that is not a charismatic gift but is common to every Christian; the reference is to wonder-working faith [cf 13:2].

4–5. gifts of healing and **the working of miracles** That both these gifts were a marked feature of the ministry of Paul and the other apostles is amply illustrated in Dr. Luke's history of the early church [for 'healings': see *Acts* 4:22, 30; 9:40; 19:11, 12; 28:7–9; and cf 2 *Cor* 12:12]. With regard to 'miracles' Calvin inclined to the view that these were the powers by which the apostles subdued demons and executed judgment upon hypocrites or evil-doers [cf *Acts* 5:1–11, 13:11, 16:18].

6. prophecy Until the canon of Scripture was complete, the New Testament prophets exercised an important ministry in the primitive church [14:29–32; *Eph* 4:11]. Prophecy, while employing the intellect, 'has a deeper seat; it is no branch of wisdom or knowledge as though coming by rational insight, but an unveiling of hidden things of God realized through a peculiar clearness and intensity of *faith*, and is in line therefore with the miraculous powers preceding; hence "the prophet" is regularly distinguished from "the teacher"' (Findlay).

7. **discernings of spirits** The 'Lord graciously provided for his churches, that some among them should be enabled in an extraordinary manner to discern and judge of them who pretended unto extraordinary actings of the Spirit. And upon the ceasing of extraordinary gifts really given from God, the gift also of discerning spirits ceased, and we are left unto the *word alone* for the trial of any that shall pretend unto them' (John Owen, 'Discourse on the Holy Spirit', *Works*, Vol. 3, p. 35).

8–9. *divers* **kinds of tongues** and **the interpretation of tongues** The fact that these spectacular gifts are completely ignored in the later Epistles suggests that even in the apostolic period they were soon displaced by a more disciplined form of worship which was offered according to recognized 'canons' (cf Ralph P. Martin, *Worship in the Early Church*, p. 137). It is clear from 14:14–16 that the man who speaks in tongues addresses God under the influence of profound emotion, 'which causes him to *pray*, *sing* or *give thanks* in an ecstatic language unintelligble to every one who does not share the same emotion, and to which his own understanding, his *nous*, remains a stranger' (Godet).

The interpretation of these mysterious utterances therefore also called for a special gift from the Spirit who had inspired them. Paul forbade tongue-speaking in church unless someone with the gift of interpretation were present, for otherwise the congregation would remain unedified by it [14:19, 27, 28].

'The extraordinary gifts of the Spirit, such as the gift of

tongues, of miracles, of prophecy, etc., are called extraordinary, because they are such as are not given in the ordinary course of God's providence. They are not bestowed in the way of God's ordinary providential dealing with his children, but only on extraordinary occasions, as they were bestowed on the prophets and apostles to enable them to reveal the mind and will of God before the canon of Scripture was complete, and so on the primitive church, in order to the founding and establishing of it in the world. But since the canon of Scripture has been completed, and the Christian church fully founded and established, these extraordinary gifts have ceased. But the ordinary gifts of the Spirit are such as are continued to the church of God throughout all ages; such gifts as are granted in conviction and conversion, and such as appertain to the building up of the saints in holiness and comfort' (Jonathan Edwards, *Charity and its Fruits*, pp. 29–30).

V11: but all these worketh the one and the same Spirit, dividing to each one severally even as he will.

All these varied gifts are the work of the *one* Spirit, who suits them to their recipients by individually distributing that which is appropriate to each one in accordance with his own wise will. Paul's insistence upon the sovereign discrimination of the Spirit in the bestowal of spiritual gifts is directed against the envy and pride which these 'inequalities' had provoked among the factious Corinthians [cf 4:7].

V12: For as the body is one, and hath many members, and all the members of the body, being many, are one body; so also is Christ.

As one life flows through all the members of the human body, so all the members of the mystical body of Christ 'are instinct with one personality' (Edwards). Paul's elaboration of this bold

[175]

figure in the following verses is intended to teach the Corinthians that as the healthy functioning of the natural body demands the harmonious working together of all its constituent parts, so it is also with the church which is the spiritual body of Christ. The unexpected substitution of 'Christ' for that body which exists only in virtue of its relationship to him, does not identify the church with the Divine-human person of Christ, but rather points all believers to him as the common source of their spiritual life. It 'shows how realistic was Paul's conception of believers as subsisting "in Christ", and raises the idea of Church-unity to its highest point' (Findlay).

*V*13 : **For in one Spirit were we all baptized into one body, whether Jews or Greeks, whether bond or free; and were all made to drink of one Spirit.**

Paul can furnish an additional proof of the oneness of the many 'in Christ' by an appeal to the experience of the Corinthians. It was because they were all baptized in one Spirit that those who were once separated from one another by differences of race and rank now formed one body. In representing the Spirit as the element in which this baptism took place, the apostle refers to the spiritual reality of which their baptism in water was the symbol. This verse therefore makes it 'difficult to resist the conclusion that the baptism of the Spirit is not a second and subsequent experience, enjoyed by some Christians, but the initial experience enjoyed by all' (John Stott, *Baptism and Fullness*, p. 39).

and were all made to drink of one Spirit. There is of course no reference to the Lord's Supper, for the verb again 'points to *a past event*, not a repeated act . . . . The two aorists describe the same primary experience under opposite figures (the former of which is *acted* in baptism), as an outward affusion and an inward absorption; the Corinthians were at once *immersed in* (cf "we were buried with", *Rom* 6:4) and *saturated with* the Spirit; the second figure supplements the first: cf *Rom* 5:5; *Tit* 3:5, 6' (Findlay).

*V*14: **For the body is not one member, but many.**

Paul is now ready to develop the figure of the body in the interest of demonstrating that each member of it exists for the good of the whole [cf *v* 7]. He insists that the various differences between the members are purely functional; they are not qualitative or 'spiritual'. Hence when all are necessary, there is no need for any member to feel inferior [*vv* 15, 20], and no cause for any member to feel superior [*vv* 21–25].

*V*15: **If the foot shall say, Because I am not the hand, I am not of the body; it is not therefore not of the body.**
*V*16: **And if the ear shall say, Because I am not the eye, I am not of the body; it is not therefore not of the body.**

'In each case it is the inferior limb which grumbles, the hand being of more value than the foot, and the eye than the ear. And Chrysostom remarks that the foot contrasts itself with the hand rather than with the ear, because we do not envy those who are very much higher than ourselves so much as those who have got a little above us' (Robertson – Plummer).

it is not therefore not of the body. This is not a question as in the AV, but an emphatic statement. 'The foot or ear does not sever itself from the body by distinguishing itself from the hand or eye; its pettish argument leaves it where it was' (Findlay).

*V*17: **If the whole body were an eye, where were the hearing? If the whole were hearing, where were the smelling?**

This is a graphic way of saying that the very existence of the body *as a body* entirely depends upon each member fulfilling the function for which it was designed. So since every member is needed by the body, none should belittle its own rôle or covet that of another. In other words, our unity in *grace* is expressed through a diversity of *gifts*.

*V*18: **But now hath God set the members each one of them in the body, even as it pleased him.**

The verse marks a return to reality, for every sane person knows that the human body did not come into being by a spontaneous process of self-development! Each member was given its particular place and function within the body by the creative act of God. 'The eye did not give itself the power of vision, nor the ear its ability to discriminate sounds. Each member occupies in the body the position which God has seen fit to assign it, and which is the most conducive to the good of the whole' (Hodge).

*V*19: **And if they were all one member, where were the body?**
*V*20: **But now they are many members, but one body.**

If the whole were one member, it would be a monstrosity and not a body! Every member is important because all are required to enable the body to function as an organic unity. 'In *v* 18 the apostle represents the various members as being, so to speak, *inserted* in the body; in verse 19 he represents the body itself as having no organic existence without its members' (Edwards).

*V*21: **And the eye cannot say to the hand, I have no need of thee: or again the head to the feet, I have no need of you.**

'Up to this point Paul has been showing what the duty of the less honourable members is, viz. to give their services to the body, and not to be envious of the more outstanding members. Now, on the other hand, he is instructing the worthier members not to despise the inferior ones, for they cannot do without them. The eye is a superior part to the hand, yet it cannot treat it with disdain, or scoff at it as a useless thing' (Calvin).

*V*22: **Nay, much rather, those members of the body which seem to be more feeble are necessary:**

'Nay more, the instant we reflect, we are convinced of the absolute *necessity* of the members which seem to play an altogether secondary part, more secondary even than the hand or the feet. These *weak* parts are no doubt the sensitive organs which are protected by their position in the body, the lungs and stomach, for example, on which, above all, the life and health of the whole body depend' (Godet).

*V*23: **and those *parts* of the body, which we think to be less honourable, upon these we bestow more abundant honour; and our uncomely *parts* have more abundant comeliness;** *v* 24: **whereas our comely *parts* have no need:**

'To bestow honour is to put on a covering for the sake of adornment, so that the parts whose exposure would be a shameful thing are decently hidden' (Calvin).

*V*24b: **but God tempered the body together, giving more abundant honour to that *part* which lacked;** *v* 25: **that there should be no schism in the body; but *that* the members should have the same care one for another.**

In creation God blended together the members of the human body in order that there should be no division of interests within it. This equality was secured when he assigned indispensable functions to its humbler members, for in so doing he bestowed more abundant honour on those parts which were naturally lacking in it. Thus all the members have the same mutual interest in caring for one another, namely, the well-being of that body to which they all belong. Paul is confident that the contentious Corinthians will have no difficulty in discerning the drift of his argument.

*V*26: **And whether one member suffereth, all the members suffer with it; or *one* member is honoured, all the members rejoice with it.**

Paul finds a further proof of the unity of the body in the mutual suffering and rejoicing of its members. As to the first, it is evident that when a finger is in pain the whole body suffers with it. And Chrysostom provides a fine illustration of the second: 'When the head is crowned, the whole man feels itself glorified; when the mouth speaks, the eyes laugh and are filled with gladness'. But in the church at Corinth this law of sympathy was conspicuous by its absence. Paul's analogy shows 'how unnatural, abnormal, unreasonable, outrageous it is for the members of the spiritual body of Christ to act in contravention of the very constitution of their own body' (Lenski).

*V*27: **Now ye are the body of Christ, and severally members thereof.**

Paul concludes the argument with this comprehensive statement. The Corinthians must understand that they sustain the same kind of relation to Christ as that which has been set forth in the preceding analogy. For as they all collectively form the body of Christ, so each is individually a member of it. 'None can claim to be the whole, but none is excluded' (Morris).

*V*28: **And God hath set some in the church, first apostles, secondly prophets, thirdly teachers, then miracles, then**

gifts of healings, helps, governments, *divers* kinds of tongues.

This begins the apostle's application of the teaching. Just as in the case of the human body, the position of every member within the spiritual organism rests solely upon the appointment of God. The enumeration, first, secondly, thirdly, distinguishes the three outstanding forms of service from five other less useful functions (so Hans Conzelmann). 'Man may appoint men to offices for which they have not the necessary gifts, but God never does, any more than he ordains the foot to see or the hand to hear. If any man, therefore, claims to be an apostle, or prophet, or worker of miracles, without the corresponding gift, he is a false pretender. In the early church, as now, there were many false apostles, i.e. those who claimed the honour and authority of the office without its gifts' (Hodge).

1–2. **apostles, prophets** As in *Eph* 4:11 these are placed first as being of the greatest importance, for it is upon the foundation of their testimony to Christ that the church is built [*Eph* 2:20]. 'The distinguishing features of an apostle were, a commission directly from Christ: being a witness of the resurrection: special inspiration: supreme authority: accrediting by miracles: unlimited commission to preach and to found churches' (Marvin Vincent). The prophets of the New Testament period were also extraordinarily endowed and exercised an unrepeatable function in that they spoke under the direct inspiration of the Spirit, 'and prior to the completion of the canon they stood to those early churches in such a relation as the written oracles stand to us' (John Eadie).

3. **teachers** Whereas *apostles* were 'rendered infallible as teachers and rulers by the plenary gift of inspiration', and

prophets 'spoke for God as the occasional organs of the Spirit'; *teachers* were 'uninspired men who had received the gift of teaching' (Hodge). Their function was therefore similar to present day ministers [cf *Eph* 4:11: 'pastors and teachers'].

4–5. then miracles, then gifts of healings, This placing is striking. Those who had these gifts are ranked below teachers, for though teaching is less dazzling than working miracles, it is more edifying. And the building up of the community is the supreme criterion of the usefulness of any gift [14:12, 26].

6–7. helps, governments Perhaps Paul refers to the ministry of mercy, and the task of church government. 'But when we boil it all down, we *know* nothing about these gifts or their possessors. They have vanished without leaving visible trace' (Leon Morris, *Spirit of the Living God*, p. 63).

8. *divers* kinds of tongues 'Last and least' (Edwards). The exciting gift upon which the Corinthians set such store is again firmly placed at the bottom of the list.

*V*29: **Are all apostles? are all prophets? are all teachers? are all *workers of* miracles? 30: have all gifts of healings? do all speak with tongues? do all interpret?**

Evidently not! But evidently some in Corinth begged to differ from the apostle and thought otherwise. Hence his unwearied insistence upon the fact that all do not speak in tongues. 'All are not, nor can be, any more than all the body can be an ear, or an eye, or a hand, or a foot: you cannot expect, that in a governed body all should be governors; and you see by experience, that all cannot work miracles, prophesy, speak with tongues, or heal those that are sick' (Poole).

*V*31a: **But desire earnestly the greater gifts.**

But though these gifts are sovereignly bestowed, Paul sees no inconsistency in urging the Corinthians to 'strive for the more valuable gifts' (Arndt-Gingrich). And it is in line with this exhortation that he urges them to seek the gift of prophecy rather than tongues [cf 14:1-5, 19]. The second part of this verse is placed at the head of the next chapter which it serves to introduce.

CHAPTER THIRTEEN

Paul now proceeds to show the only way in which spiritual gifts can be fruitfully exercised. For without love the greatest gifts are worthless [vv 12:31b–13:3]. Love inspires and animates every grace, as it also excludes every form of sinful self-assertiveness [vv 4–7]. And in contrast to temporary gifts, love, with faith and hope, will last for ever [vv 8–13].

*V*12:31b: **And moreover a most excellent way show I unto you.**

Paul is not drawing a contrast between love and gifts, but is showing that love is the only way in which gifts can be effectively exercised. For gifts are nothing without the grace of love. The Christian Way is pre-eminently the way of love. This is something which had been sadly overlooked in Corinth.

*V*1: **If I speak with the tongues of men and of angels, but have not love, I am become sounding brass, or a clanging cymbal.**

Paul here first mentions what he considers to be 'last and least' of the gifts because of the Corinthians' exaggerated estimate of its importance. 'According to the Corinthian measuring of the ecstatic life, glossolalia (or tongues) comes first as heavenly speech' (H. Conzelmann, *TDNT*, Vol. IX,

p. 405). He compares the loveless exercise of this gift to the meaningless sounds produced by a noisy gong or a clanging cymbal (instruments which were used to excite the worshippers in the ecstatic cults of Demeter and Cybele). For without love the most impressive display of religious emotion is of no value. And in his insistence upon this truth, Paul is not a whit behind the Apostle of love himself [cf 1 *John*; *Rom* 13:8–10; *Gal* 5:6; 1 *Thess* 3:12, etc.].

V2: **And if I have** *the gift of* **prophecy, and know all mysteries and all knowledge; and if I have all faith, so as to remove mountains, but have not love, I am nothing.**

Paul further supposes that if he should have the gift of prophecy in such a degree that his inspired insight into all the mysteries of God were matched by an exhaustive intellectual knowledge of them, and that if he should have such wonder-working faith that he could remove mountains (an evident allusion to the Lord's teaching, cf *Matt* 17:20), yet even all these powers could not make up for the absence of love in the heart.

I am nothing. Paul's abrupt conclusion of his extended hypothesis brings out the utter destitution of the graceless man, notwithstanding his possession of the most extraordinary gifts. 'Salvation is promised to those who have the graces of the Spirit, but not to those who have merely the extraordinary gifts. Many may have these last, and yet go to hell. Judas Iscariot had them, and is gone to hell. And Christ tells us, that many who have them, will, at the last day, be bid to depart, as workers of iniquity [*Matt* 7:22, 23]. And therefore, when he promised his disciples these extraordinary gifts, he bade them rejoice, not because the devils were subject to them, but because their names were written in heaven; intimating that the one might be, and yet not the other [*Luke* 10:17]. And this shows that the one is an infinitely greater blessing than the other, as it carries eternal life in it' (Jonathan Edwards).

*V*3 : **And if I bestow all my goods to feed** *the poor*, **and if I give my body to be burned, but have not love, it profiteth me nothing.**

Paul next exposes the vanity of every form of self-sacrifice which stops short of surrendering the self to God [2 *Cor* 8:5]. 'Natural unrenewed men would be glad to have something to make up for the want of sincere love and real grace in their hearts; and many do great things to make up for the want of it, while others are willing to suffer great things. But, alas! how little does it all signify!' (Jonathan Edwards).

And if I should give away in doles of food all my possessions, (Robertson – Plummer). Without love, even such a reckless disposition of one's property would not suffice to extinguish the egoism which prompted its seemingly selfless distribution.

and if I give my body to be burned, but have not love, Even to embrace a martyr's death is of no value 'if it is finally orientated to self rather than to God . . . Heroic religious achievements can become a false righteousneess of works in which grace is no longer all in all. The desire for one's own cross in martyrdom can obscure the cross of Christ' (K. L. Schmidt, *TDNT*, Vol. III, p. 466).

it profiteth me nothing. This is here substituted for the 'I am nothing' of *v* 2, 'because now it is not the worth of the person but of the acts which is in question. What was intended to assure me of salvation, has no value in the eyes of God, whenever the object of it becomes self, in the form of self-merit or of human glory. Love accepts only what is inspired by love' (Godet).

*V*4: **Love suffereth long, *and* is kind; love envieth not; love vaunteth not itself, is not puffed up, *v* 5: doth not behave itself unseemly, seeketh not its own, is not provoked, taketh not account of evil; *v* 6: rejoiceth not in unrighteousness, but rejoiceth with the truth; *v* 7: beareth all things, believeth all things, hopeth all things, endureth all things.**

The behaviour of Love is set forth in 'fifteen exquisite aphorisms', which says Findlay, 'run in seven couplets, arranged as one positive, four negative, and two positive verse-lines . . . The paragraph then reads as follows:

> "*Love suffers long, shows kindness.*
> *Love envies not, makes no self-display;*
> *Is not puffed up, behaves not unseemly;*
> *Seeks not her advantage, is not embittered;*
> *Imputes not evil, rejoices not at wrong,*
> *but shares in the joy of the truth.*
> *All things she tolerates, all things she believes;*
> *All things she hopes for, all things she endures.*"'

This description of love is directly opposed to the spirit in which the Corinthians exercised their gifts. 'The lyric is thus a lancet. Paul is probing for some of the diseases that were weakening the body spiritual at Corinth' (Moffatt).

1. **Love suffereth long,** 'Love to God disposes us to *imitate* him, and therefore disposes us to such long-suffering as he manifests . . . The long-suffering of God is very wonderfully manifest in his bearing innumerable injuries from men, and injuries that are very great and long-continued' (Jonathan Edwards) [*Exod* 34:6; *Rom* 2:4].

2. *and* is kind; Such 'was predominantly the character of Christ's ministry, which dispensed deeds of gentle kindness among all the lowly and the needy with whom he came in contact. Thus to God-like "longsuffering" there is added Christ-like "benignity"' (Lenski). [*Acts* 10:38]

3. **love envieth not;** The opposite positive quality is implied in the eight negatives which follow the first couplet. 'Envy may be defined to be a spirit of dissatisfaction with, and opposition to, the prosperity and happiness of others as compared with our own' (Jonathan Edwards). [*Num* 11:29]

4. **love vaunteth not itself,** Love is no 'braggart' or 'wind-bag' (Arndt-Gingrich). 'Behind boastful bragging there lies conceit, an overestimation of one's own importance, abilities, or achievements' (Lenski). [*Phil* 2:3, 4]

5. **is not puffed up,** The Corinthians' besetting sin [cf 4:6, 18, 19; 5:2; 8.1]. 'There are many ways of manifesting pride; and love is incompatible with them all. Love is concerned rather to give itself than to assert itself' (Morris).

6. **doth not behave itself unseemly,** Love's behaviour is not contrary to the 'form, fashion, or manner that is proper. When pride puffs up the heart, unseemly bearing and conduct naturally follow' (Lenski). [cf. 11:6–15, 14:40]

7. **seeketh not its own,** 'Love not merely does not seek that which does not belong to it; it is prepared to give up for the sake of others even what it is entitled to' (Barrett). [10:24, 33]

8. **is not provoked,** 'Not merely "does not fly into a rage", but "does not yield to provocation": it is not embittered by injuries, whether real or supposed' (Robertson – Plummer). [*Gal* 5:22, 23]

9. **taketh not account of evil;** 'Love, instead of entering evil as a debt in its account book, voluntarily passes the sponge over what it endures' (Godet). [cf *Philem* 18]

10. **rejoiceth not in unrighteousness,** 'To "rejoice at iniquity", when seeing it in others, is a sign of deep debasement [*Rom* 1:32]' (Findlay).

11. **but rejoiceth with the truth;** The last negative proposition is rounded off with its positive counterpart because Love must take sides with the Truth, which is here personified. 'The false charity which compromises "the truth" by glossing over "iniquity" is thus condemned [*Prov* 17:15]' (Fausset). [cf *Eph* 4:15]

12. **covers all things,** Arndt-Gingrich give the first meaning of the word *stegō* as '*cover, pass over in silence, keep confidential*', and say that in this verse it refers to 'love that throws a cloak of silence over what is displeasing in another person'.

13. **believeth all things,** 'All that is not palpably false, all that it can with a good conscience believe to the credit of another' (Fausset). [cf *Philem* 21]

14. **hopeth all things,** While the first pair of 'all things' relate to present experience, the second look more to the future. Here the 'thought is not that of unreasoning optimism, which fails to take account of reality. It is rather a refusal to take failure as final' (Morris). [2 *Cor* 1:7]

15. **endureth all things.** This 'is that cheerful and loyal fortitude which, having done all without apparent success, still stands and endures, whether the ingratitude of friends or the persecution of foes' (Robertson – Plummer). [*Eph* 6:13]

*V*8: **Love never faileth: but whether *there be* prophecies they shall be done away; whether *there be* tongues, they**

[189]

shall cease; whether *there be* **knowledge, it shall be done away.**

Love never ends; (RSV). Love never comes to an end. While the gifts of the Spirit are a *means* of grace, divine love is *grace itself*, 'and therefore remains when the means to it cease' (Jonathan Edwards). The argument shifts here to direct polemic. In the previous verses Paul has said that gifts are nothing without love. But now love and spiritual gifts are set in opposition to each other, because gifts are *temporary* whereas love is *eternal*. Thus in contrast to the Corinthians who regarded these gifts as the sign that they had already attained the glories of heaven [cf *v* 1 with 4:8], Paul insists that the possession of the gifts is the proof positive that they are still held fast in the 'not yet' of spiritual immaturity (so Conzelmann).

prophecies . . . tongues . . . knowledge These – 'faculties inspired, ecstatic, intellectual – are the three typical forms of Christian expression. The abolition of Prophecies and Knowledge is explained in *vv* 9ff as the superseding of the partial by the perfect; they "will be done away" by a completer realization of the objects they seek, – viz., by *intuition* into the now hidden things of God and of man [14:24f], and by adequate *comprehension* of the things revealed. Of the Tongues it is simply said that 'they will *stop*', having like other miracles a temporary significance [cf 14:22]; not giving place to any higher development of the like kind, they lapse and terminate' (Findlay).

*V*9: **For we know in part, and we prophesy in part;** *v* 10: **but when that which is perfect is come, that which is in part shall be done away.**

Our present knowledge is imperfect because it is partial. This is an imperfection of degree rather than quality. What we know of God by revelation is indeed truly known, for it is infallibly communicated. But when this fragmentary disclosure at last gives place to the beatific vision of God in Christ, then 'that which is in part shall be done away'.

*V*11: **When I was a child, I spake as a child, I felt as a child, I thought as a child: now that I am become a man, I have put away childish things.**

Our progress from infancy to maturity serves to illustrate this truth [*vv* 9, 10]. Paul does not deny that the child is father to the man, for he was the same 'I' in childhood as he is now in manhood; he merely asserts that as a man he has no desire to become a child again. This means that just as the adult sets aside the nature of the child, so the Christian sets aside the knowledge which seems to be essential now, i.e. in the stage of infancy (so G. Bertram, *TDNT*, Vol. IV, p. 919). So though even now we are sons of God, yet we are still little children. Our present views of divine things are not untrue but inadequate. Hereafter things will be very different. 'It is no part of the apostle's object to unsettle our confidence in what God now communicates by his word and Spirit to his children, but simply to prevent our being satisfied with the partial and imperfect' (Hodge).

*V*12: **For now we see in a mirror, darkly; but then face to face: now I know in part; but then shall I know fully even as also I was fully known.**

Paul's figure is based on the familiar Old Testament contrast between the ordinary prophets, whose knowledge of the Lord was mediated through visions and dreams, and Moses to whom the Lord directly manifested himself [*Num* 12:8]. So at present our knowledge of God is indirect: 'we only see the baffling reflections in a mirror' (Moffatt). 'Our present understanding is like peering into a primitive metal mirror with its imperfect reflection [cf 2 *Cor* 5:7]. But then, in the next life, we shall see face to face [cf 1 *John* 3:2]' (Hillyer). Since such mirrors were made in Corinth Paul's readers would be quick to grasp the point [cf 2 *Cor* 3:18].

but then shall I know fully even as also I have been known fully. (RV margin) 'As God's direct and all-penetrating knowledge takes into account every one of his children already in eternity and, of course, through all of life, so we, too, shall at last know God directly and completely to the highest degree in which this is possible for his children' (Lenski).

*V*13: **But now abideth faith, hope, love, these three; and the greatest of these is love.**

Paul concludes by saying that when every gift has passed away [*vv* 8ff], this well-known triad of Christian virtues eternally abides [*Rom* 5:1-5; *Gal* 5, 6; 1 *Thess* 1:3, 5:8]. But, asks Alford, how can *faith* and *hope* be said to endure to eternity, when faith will be lost in sight, and hope in fruition? With *hope* there is but little difficulty. 'New glories, new treasures of knowledge and of love, will ever raise, and nourish, blessed hopes of yet more and higher, – hopes which no disappointment will blight. But how can *faith* abide, – faith, which is the evidence of things *not seen*, where all things once believed are seen? In the form of *holy confidence and trust*, faith will abide even there. The stay of all conscious created being, human or angelic, is *dependence on God*; and where the faith which *comes by hearing* is out of the question, the faith which *consists of trusting* will be the only faith possible. Thus *Hope* will remain, as anticipation certain to be fulfilled: *Faith* will remain, as trust, entire and undoubting: the anchor of the soul, even where no tempest comes'.

but the greatest of these is love. (RSV) Of these eternal virtues love is the greatest, because love alone is divine. 'God does not believe nor hope, but he loves. Love belongs to his essence. Like God himself, it could not change its nature except for the worse. Love is the end in relation to which the two other virtues are only means, and this relation remains even in the state of perfection' (Godet). [1 *John* 4:16, 19]

CHAPTER FOURTEEN

Provided the Corinthians follow the way of love, they are right to desire spiritual gifts, but they should seek prophecy rather than tongues [vv 1–5]. For unless tongues are interpreted, they are mere sounds without meaning, and so bring no benefit to the hearers [vv 6–11]. Because the edification of the church is the standard by which all gifts are to be measured, Paul would rather speak five intelligible words to instruct others than ten thousand in an unknown tongue [vv 12–19]. It was therefore childish to prefer an incomprehensible utterance which hindered the worship of the church to a rational message that helped it [vv 20–25]. In public worship Paul forbids tongues unless an interpreter is present, and then no more than two or three may speak in turn. The prophets must also wait their turn to speak, for God is not the author of confusion [vv 26–33]. Women are not to speak at all in church, but must save any questions for their husbands at home [vv 34, 35]. As the gospel did not originate in Corinth, they are not a law unto themselves, and must see that all things are done decently and in order [vv 36–40].

VI: **Follow after love; yet desire earnestly spiritual gifts, but rather that ye may prophesy.**

The enthusiasm for tongues in Corinth made it necessary for Paul to prepare the ground carefully before dealing specifically with the disorders which had resulted from the indisciplined use of this gift. But having demonstrated the primacy of love, he is now ready to give his practical directions for the orderly conduct of public worship. He sums up the teaching of the previous chapter in the crisp command, 'Pursue after love'. Parry points out that this is a favourite metaphor with Paul for spiritual effort [cf *Rom* 9:30, 31; 12:13; *Phil* 3:12f; 1 *Thess* 5:15; 1 *Tim* 6:11; 2 *Tim* 2:22]. If the Corinthians get their priorities right and put love first, they may indeed eagerly desire spiritual gifts, but they will seek the gift of prophecy rather than tongues. Throughout this extended discussion Paul's point-by-point demonstration of the inferiority of tongues to prophecy 'is such as to pour a douche of ice-cold water over the whole practice' (H. Chadwick cited by F. F. Bruce). The predictive element is not emphasized in the gift of prophecy as it appears here (in contrast to Agabus, cf *Acts* 11:28, 21:10): it is *inspired* forthtelling rather than fore-telling. 'Modern *preaching* is its successor, without the inspiration. Desire zealously this (prophecy) more than any other spiritual gift, especially *in preference to* 'tongues', [*vv* 2ff]' (Fausset). However, both tongues and prophecy were *speech*, and this shows that Paul gives no place for any gathering together in *silence*, not even in *v* 30.

*V*2: **For he that speaketh in a tongue speaketh not unto men, but unto God; for no man understandeth; but in the spirit he speaketh mysteries.**

This gives the reason for preferring prophecy. It is that the man who speaks with tongues brings no benefit to his fellow-believers [cf *Eph* 4:29], for though *God* understands what he says no one else can [*v* 9]! 'There was *sound* enough in the glossolalia [13:1], but no sense [*v* 23]' (Findlay).

but in the spirit he speaketh mysteries. *V*14 makes it clear that the reference must be to the spirit of the believer as distinguished from his understanding. The ecstatic utterance of such mysteries was therefore a revelation [see note on 2:7], which stopped 'short of disclosure tantalizing the church, which hears and hears not' (Findlay).

*V*3: But he that prophesieth speaketh unto men edification, and exhortation, and consolation.

But he who prophesies speaks to *men*, and his intelligible words are a means of edification (or 'building up': see on 8:1), for they serve to encourage and comfort others. Paul uses the terms 'edification' and 'to edify' no less than seven times in ch 14 [*vv* 3–5, 12, 26; *vv* 4 (twice), 17], and this shows that he 'subjects all events of worship to the single and clear criterion of the "edification" of the congregation' (G. Bornkamm, *Early Christian Experience*, pp. 162–163).

*V*4: He that speaketh in a tongue edifieth himself; but he that prophesieth edifieth the church.

There is a striking contrast between the speaker in a tongue who edifies only himself, and the prophet who edifies the whole church. Paul is attacking the selfish individualism of the Corinthians. It is 'wrong for the man who speaks in tongues to edify himself [*v* 4]. This act is not orientated to the community and the brother [*v* 17], it is not regarded as service, and consequently it is not dictated by love, but is self-directed' (O. Michel, *TDNT*, Vol. V, p. 141).

*V*5: Now I would have you all speak with tongues, but rather that ye should prophesy: and greater is he that prophesieth than he that speaketh with tongues,

except he interpret, that the church may receive edifying.

It is not through any spirit of antipathy or jealousy that Paul so speaks of tongues, for he speaks with tongues more than they all [*v* 18]. His aim is rather to help the Corinthians properly to estimate the value of this gift. Although he would have them all speak with tongues, yet it would be even better for them to have the gift of prophecy, because the man who prophesies is 'greater' than he who speaks in a tongue, unless of course he also has the ability to interpret his utterance for the benefit of the congregation. In that case he would do 'in two acts what the prophet does in one' (Findlay).

*V*6: **But now, brethren, if I come unto you speaking with tongues, what shall I profit you, unless I speak to you either by way of revelation, or of knowledge, or of prophesying, or of teaching?**

Knowing their exaggerated esteem for tongues, Paul asks the Corinthians to judge what spiritual benefit they would receive from him if he should come to them speaking only in tongues. Would they now be his 'brethren' in Christ, if on his first visit to Corinth he had merely appeared in their midst as a demented ecstatic? [cf *v* 23]. Was it not by means of an address to their understanding in comprehensible speech that the light of the gospel had dawned upon them? [2:2]. And did they now expect to reach Christian maturity by exalting to the premier place a gift which left their highest faculty unedified? [*v* 14]. 'There are not four, but only two modes of address contemplated in this verse. Revelation and prophecy belong to one; and knowledge and doctrine to the other. He who received revelations was a prophet, he who had "the word of knowledge" was a teacher' (Hodge).

*V*7: **Even things without life, giving a voice, whether**

pipe or harp, if they give not a distinction in the sounds, how shall it be known what is piped or harped?

Paul next illustrates the importance of intelligibility by three examples: 1. musical instruments [*v* 7]; 2. military trumpet and application [*vv* 8, 9]; 3. human language and application [*vv* 10, 11]. 'Paul says, "Even the very inanimate things teach us a lesson". Of course there are many noises or crashes to be heard by chance, which have no musical significance. But Paul is speaking here about sounds which are the products of certain technical skill, as though he said: "A man cannot give life to a harp or flute, but he produces sounds, which are adjusted in such a way that they can be picked out. How absurd then that actual men, endowed as they are with intelligence, should utter indistinguishable and unintelligible sounds!" ' (Calvin). But some instruments cannot produce a melody and make only a noise, and in 13:1 Paul significantly compares those who speak in tongues with the unmeaning crash of gong and cymbals (so Héring).

*V*8: **For if the trumpet give an uncertain voice, who shall prepare himself for war?**
*V*9: **So also ye, unless ye utter by the tongue speech easy to be understood, how shall it be known what is spoken? for ye will be speaking into the air.**

The use of the trumpet in the military realm was well known to Jews and Greeks alike. But if the trumpet is not blown to give notice of a pre-arranged signal, then not only is its message meaningless, but the lives of the troops who hear it are thereby placed in jeopardy. Paul is stressing the fact that the mere delivery of sound without sense is worse than useless. So the man whose words cannot be understood in church is simply 'speaking into the air'. The use of such a down-to-earth proverbial phrase is very forceful. It is like saying, He is wasting his breath!

*V*10: **There are, it may be, so many kinds of voices in the world, and no *kind* is without signification.**

Paul has no idea how many languages there are in the world, but he is convinced that none of them 'is without voice' (ASV margin), i.e. without meaning. Since the whole purpose of language is communication, an utterance which mystifies rather than edifies the hearers is virtually 'voiceless'. And 'meaningless sound, had better be inaudible; it is a mere distracting noise. This was just the case with Tongues in a congregation without an interpreter' (Robertson – Plummer).

*V*11: **If then I know not the meaning of the voice, I shall be to him that speaketh a barbarian, and he that speaketh will be a barbarian unto me.**

The mutual exchange of thought is impossible unless both speak the same language. Otherwise each would regard the other as a 'barbarian', i.e. someone whose speech gave the impression of being nothing more than a meaningless jumble of sounds like 'bar bar'. This derogatory connotation is not absent from Paul's thought here. 'The ecstatic speech which seemed to the Corinthians a matter for such pride turns out to be the means of making them nothing more than barbarians. This would be even worse for a Greek than for us' (Morris).

*V*12: **So also ye, since ye are zealous of spiritual *gifts*, seek that ye may abound unto the edifying of the church.**

There is a touch of irony in Paul's admission that the Corinthians are indeed zealous to obtain spiritual gifts (literally, 'spirits' pointing to the various agencies producing these various gifts, cf 12:10; 1 *John* 4:1). Yet what they have failed to grasp is that their individual distribution among them is not for private gratification or personal display (because love 'seeketh not *its own*' – 13:5), but for the *common good* of that one body to which they all belong. 'To this end prophecy should have the preponderance, or tongues be accompanied with interpretation' (Godet).

*V*13: **Wherefore let him that speaketh in a tongue pray that he may interpret.**

*V*14: **For if I pray in a tongue, my spirit prayeth, but my understanding is unfruitful.**

'Wherefore' introduces the practical application. Since the church can only be edified by hearing an intelligible message, the man who speaks in a tongue should pray that God would also grant him the ability to interpret this ecstatic utterance. In verse 14 what Paul tactfully supposes of himself condemns what the Corinthians are actually doing. 'For if I pray in a tongue, my spirit prays, but my rational faculty remains unfruitful'. His own spirit is edified, but because what is *felt* is not transformed into intelligible speech by his understanding, no benefit is communicated to the congregation. 'The *fruit* of the speaker is found in the profit of the hearer' (Theodoret). It is strange that those who so prided themselves upon their wisdom, 'should need to be told that intellect is not to be ignored, but ought to be brought to full development [*v* 20]' (Robertson – Plummer).

*V*15: **What is it then? I will pray with the spirit, and I will pray with the understanding also: I will sing with the spirit, and I will sing with the understanding also.**

'What then is the upshot of this discussion?' Because the worship of God is an exercise which engages the *whole* man, Paul is resolved to pray and sing not only with the spirit, but also with the understanding. Fervency of spirit must be found in alliance with the illumination of the intellect, and neither is acceptable without the other. 'Rational prayer is not less spiritual than irrational' (Barrett).

*V*16: **Else if thou bless with the spirit, how shall he that filleth the place of the unlearned say the Amen at thy giving of thanks, seeing he knoweth not what thou sayest?**
*V*17: **For thou verily givest thanks well, but the other is not edified.**

The man who speaks in a tongue when the church is at worship is guilty of 'unseemly' behaviour towards his fellow-believers [13:5], because his unintelligible utterance forces them into a place which is not properly theirs, viz., that of the 'unlearned' (i.e. it puts them among those who are 'uninitiated' into God's mysteries). If they could not understand a word of what was said, then it would be a meaningless mockery to express their audible assent to it by the usual 'Amen' [*Neh* 8:6]. The 'thou' and the 'well' of *v* 17 are, as Godet says, 'slightly ironical'. 'Paul estimates the devotions of the church by a spiritually utilitarian standard; the abstractly beautiful is subordinated to the practically edifying' (Findlay).

*V*18: **I thank God, I speak with tongues more than you all: 19: howbeit in the church I had rather speak five words with my understanding, that I might instruct others also, than ten thousand words in a tongue.**

It is not because Paul is himself a stranger to ecstatic experiences of this kind that he discourages tongues in public worship [cf 2 *Cor* 12:1-4]. Indeed he speaks 'with tongues *more* than you all'. He surpasses them all in this *mode of speaking*. Had he wished to point to a greater proficiency in foreign languages he would rather have said: 'Because I speak in *more* tongues than you all' (Godet). But he only exercises this gift in private, for he would prefer to speak five sensible words to instruct his fellow-Christians 'than to utter a torrent of words in a tongue' (Morris). Thus it was not through exciting emotional experiences that the apostle sought to edify the Corinthians, but by addressing a rational message to their minds. 'In presenting the Christian gospel we must never, in the first place, make a *direct* approach either to the emotions or to the will. The emotions and the will should always be influenced through the mind. Truth is intended to come to the *mind*. The normal course is for the emotions and the will to be affected by the truth after it has first entered and gripped the mind' (D. Martyn Lloyd-Jones, *Conversions: Psychological and Spiritual*, p. 39).

*V*20: **Brethren, be not children in mind: yet in malice be ye babes, but in mind be men.**

This exhortation begins a new paragraph. The affectionate address somewhat softens Paul's keen reproof. 'Emulation and love of display were betraying this church into a child-ishness the very opposite of that broad intelligence and enlightenment on which it plumed itself' (Findlay). Godet also remarks that it is 'characteristic of the child to prefer the amusing to the useful, the brilliant to the solid', and para-phrases the verse thus: 'If you will be children, well and good, provided it be in malice; but as to understanding, advance more and more toward full maturity'.

*V*21: **In the law it is written, By men of strange tongues and by the lips of strangers will I speak unto this people; and not even thus will they hear me, saith the Lord.**

Paul next introduces a free quotation of *Is* 28:11, 12 to illustrate the danger of despising a clear revelation (prophecy) in favour of an unintelligible utterance (tongues). 'According to the true interpretation of *Is* 28:7ff, the drunken Israelites are mocking in their cups the teaching of God through his prophet, as though it were only fit for an infant school; in anger therefore he threatens to give his lessons through the lips of foreign conquerors (11), in whose speech the despisers of the mild, plain teaching of his servants (12) shall painfully spell out their ruin . . . God spoke to Israel through the strange Assyrian tongue *in retribution*, not to confirm their faith but to consummate their unbelief. The Glossolalia (speaking with tongues) may serve a similar melancholy purpose in the church' (Findlay).

*V*22: **Wherefore tongues are for a sign, not to them that believe, but to the unbelieving: but prophesying *is for a sign*, not to the unbelieving, but to them that believe.**

Apparently there were those in Corinth who regarded speaking in tongues as 'a sign' for believers, i.e. as a proof of their superior spiritual standing and authority. But according to Paul's application of this Old Testament quotation tongues are not a sign of divine pleasure but of divine judgment. For if the Corinthians persist in their perverse preference for the obscure phenomenon of tongues, then they must not be surprised if their unbelieving rejection of prophecy is judicially confirmed by God. 'Paul desires to quench rather than stimulate the Corinthian ardour for Tongues' (Findlay).

but prophesying is for a sign, not to the unbelieving, but to them that believe. 'It is wholly otherwise with prophetic exhortations. These are a sign of faith or of the disposition to believe which already exists in those to whom God thus speaks' (Godet).

*V*23: **If therefore the whole church be assembled together and all speak with tongues, and there come in men unlearned or unbelieving, will they not say that ye are mad?**

This vividly depicts the disastrous impression which the unbridled exercise of tongues in church would make upon the outsider ('unlearned' here appears without the qualification of *v* 16) and upon the unbeliever who came to the service to learn something about the Christian faith. Paul's point is that what outsiders find completely meaningless cannot edify the church; whereas that which builds up the church also serves to convict and convert outsiders [*vv* 24, 25]. 'If the Tongues are, as many Corinthians think, the highest manifestation of the Spirit, then to have the whole church simultaneously so speaking would be the *ne plus ultra* of spiritual power; but, in fact, the church would then resemble nothing so much as a congregation of lunatics! A *reductio ad absurdum* for the fanatical coveters of Tongues' (Findlay).

*V*24: **But if all prophesy, and there come in one unbelieving or unlearned, he is reproved by all, he is judged by all;** *v* 25: **the secrets of his heart are made manifest; and so he will fall down on his face and worship God, declaring that God is among you indeed.**

Tongues may succeed in arousing the scorn of the unbeliever, but only prophecy can make him a believer; a blessedly different result which justifies Paul's critical appraisal of the relative value of these gifts. It is by this inspired preaching that the presence of God among his people is validated in the experience of the unbeliever, for it subjects his inner life to a moral illumination which convicts him of his sin, leads to self-condemnation, and issues in submission to God [cf *Heb* 4:12]. 'What passes in him at such a moment resembles what passed in Paul on the way to Damascus. Struck by this light, he casts himself in the dust, not before man, but before God, acknowledging that such brightness can only proceed from the Holy of holies and the Searcher of hearts; that consequently it is He who speaks by the mouth of those into the midst of whom he has come' (Godet).

*V*26: **What is it then, brethren? When ye come together, each one hath a psalm, hath a teaching, hath a revelation, hath a tongue, hath an interpretation. Let all things be done unto edifying.**

Having concluded his treatment of spiritual gifts, Paul next shows how they are to be used in the church [*vv* 26–33]. These detailed directions were necessary because the abundance of gifts possessed by the Corinthians was matched by their eagerness to exercise them. Consequently, spontaneity in worship quickly degenerated into confusion and disorder. In this section Paul is at pains to point out that this unseemly and irreverent behaviour must be rectified at once [*v* 33]. E. A. Abbott expands the verse thus: 'Just when ye are assembling for sacred worship, and ought to be thinking of Christ and of Christ's body, the congregation, each one is perhaps thinking of himself, "I have a Psalm", "I have a Doctrine", "I have a Revelation". Have done with this! Let all be done to edification' (cited in Robertson – Plummer).

*V*27: **If any man speaketh in a tongue, *let it be* by two, or at the most three, and *that* in turn; and let one interpret:** *v* 28: **but if there be no interpreter, let him keep silence in the church; and let him speak to himself, and to God.**

Although there may be many in the congregation ready to speak in tongues, no more than two, or at the most three, should be allowed to do so, 'and that in turn'. Furthermore, if no interpreter is present, the tongue-speaker must keep silent in the church, and exercise his gift privately at home. For without interpretation his gift is of no value to the church. 'One, and one only (*heis* not *tis*), was to interpret; there was to be no interpreting in turn, which might lead to profitless discussion. Moreover, this would be a security against two speaking with Tongues at the same time, for one interpreter could not attend to both' (Robertson – Plummer).

*V*29: **And let the prophets speak** *by* **two or three, and let others discern.**
*V*30: **But if a revelation be made to another sitting by, let the first keep silence.**
*V*31: **For ye all can prophesy one by one, that all may learn, and all may be exhorted;**

Similarly, only two or three may prophesy at one church meeting, while those who have the gift of discernment are to judge whether their utterances are really inspired or not [cf 12:10; *Deut* 18:22; 1 *John* 4:1]. If a direct revelation is received by a prophet who has not been chosen to speak, then the appointed speaker is to give place to him. Eventually all the prophets will have their turn at speaking so that the whole congregation may learn and be strengthened by their distinctive contributions.

When these directions [*vv* 26–33] are placed in their proper historical perspective it will be seen that they cannot apply to us today, because the great lack which prophecy and tongues were intended to fill in the primitive church was supplied as soon as the canon of Scripture was complete. Therefore those who assert that the apostolic gifts are still continued in the church leave believers at the mercy of a form of sooth-saying which cannot be gainsaid because its deluded exponents claim to have received a direct revelation from the Lord! Evangelicals should face up to the fact that such a presumptuous claim places the confused utterances of uninspired men on exactly the same level as inspired Scripture. Now it is granted 'that Scripture does not continue to be written, that it is a closed canon. Once this is admitted, then we must entertain . . . that conception of Scripture taught and pre-supposed by our Lord and his apostles, and insist that it is this conception that must be applied to the whole canon of Scripture. Since we no longer have prophets, since we do not have our Lord with us as he was with the disciples, and since we do not have new organs of revelation as in apostolic times, Scripture in its total extent, according to the conception entertained by our Lord and his apostles, is the only revelation of the mind and will of God available to us. This is what the finality of Scripture means for us; it is the only extant revelatory Word of God' (John Murray, 'The Finality and Sufficiency of Scripture', *Collected Writings, Vol. I, p.* 19).

*V*32: **and the spirits of the prophets are subject to the prophets;** *v* 33a: **for God is not *a God* of confusion, but of peace.**

Unlike the diabolical inspirations of heathenism [12:2], the breathings of God's Spirit do not carry away the prophet without his consent or will, and therefore 'he has no right to make inspiration a pretext for refusing to submit to the rules laid down by the apostle' (Godet). And this must be so, for it would be the height of impiety to attribute the confusion which would result from a prophetic free-for-all to him who is the God of peace.

*V*33b: **As in all the churches of the saints,** *v* 34: **let the women keep silence in the churches: for it is not permitted unto them to speak; but let them be in subjection, as also saith the law.**
*V*35: **And if they would learn anything, let them ask their own husbands at home: for it is shameful for a woman to speak in the church.**

The church in Corinth was not a law unto itself, and was not therefore free to permit what was forbidden in other churches.

However, it is not merely on the strength of universal custom that Paul enjoins silence upon the women of Corinth during public worship; it is an authoritative command because it is of divine origin [cf *Gen* 3:16]. 'Any act on the part of woman which sets aside her subjection to man is in violation of "the Law", the will of God expressed in creation and stated in his Word. An act of such a nature would be the speaking of women in the public services either in a tongue or in prophecy ... In many places woman may speak and teach even publicly, but in no place where she will exercise "dominion over a man" by her teaching' (Lenski) [1 *Tim* 2:12–14] The prohibition is absolute and extends even to the asking of questions. This is to be done at home. It is as *shameful* a thing for a woman to speak in church as it would be to have her hair shorn (the same word as in 11:6).

'To Paul, the human race is made up of families, and every several organism, the church included, is composed of families, united together by this or that bond. The relation of the sexes in the family follows it therefore into the church. To the feminist movement the human race is made up of individuals; a woman is just another individual by the side of the man; and it can see no reason for any differences in dealing with the two. And, indeed, if we can ignore the great fundamental natural difference of sex, and destroy the great fundamental social unit of the family, in the interest of individualism, there does not seem any reason why we should not wipe out the differences established by Paul between the sexes in the church. Except, of course, the authority of Paul. It all, in the end, comes back to the authority of the apostles, as founders of the church. We may like what Paul says, or we may not like it. We may be willing to do what he commands, or we may not be willing to do it. But there is no room for doubt of what he says' (B. B. Warfield, 'Paul on Women Speaking in Church', *The Saviour of the World*, p. 267).

And we may add that if Paul's injunction had been respected and obeyed there would have been no opportunity for charlatans like Aimee Semple McPherson, Ellen G. White, and Mary Baker Eddy to have imposed their noxious wares upon a gullible public!

V36: What? was it from you that the word of God went forth? or came it unto you alone?

'Will you obey me? Or, if you set up your judgment above that of other churches, do you pretend that your church is the first FROM which the gospel came, that you should give law to all others? Or are you the only persons UNTO whom it has come?' (Fausset).

V37: If any man thinketh himself to be a prophet, or spiritual, let him take knowledge of the things which I write unto you, that they are the commandment of the Lord.

Having concluded his discussion of spiritual gifts (chs 12–14), Paul now affixes the seal of his authority to what he has written. Let anyone who thinks he is a prophet or spiritually gifted, prove his claim by acknowledging that what the apostle is writing is the *Lord's* commandment. Anyone who fails to recognize the inspiration and authority of Paul's words not only shows that he has no spiritual discernment, but also affords proof positive that he is not of God [*John* 8:47; 1 *John* 4:6).

V38: But if any man is ignorant, let him be ignorant.

But if any one is ignorant of the source of Paul's authority, he must be left to his ignorance and all it entails. An 'argument likely to have weight with the Corinthians, who admired "knowledge" so much' (Fausset).

*V*39: **Wherefore, my brethren, desire earnestly to prophesy, and forbid not to speak with tongues.**

The whole discussion is now affectionately summed up in one lucid directive [*vv* 39, 40]. Paul actively encourages the Corinthians to prophesy, but merely says that they are not to hinder speaking with tongues. 'A vast difference; the one gift to be greatly longed for, the other only not forbidden' (Robertson – Plummer).

*V*40: **But let all things be done decently and in order.**

Paul's detailed directions in this chapter on the conduct of worship applied to the special circumstances of the church in Corinth. But two principles remain regulative to this day: all things should be done for edification [*v* 26], and all things should be done decently and in order. 'The lasting importance of this chapter lies in the fact that Paul sets forth what the character of the divine service must be. That which he writes about that subject is still valid. Furthermore we learn that God the Holy Spirit had endowed the early Christians with special gifts, charismata, and that He guided the ancient church by means of them. We also notice how great the dangers connected with those gifts. That should make us grateful that in the Holy Scriptures of the Old and New Testaments we have all that we need' (Grosheide).

CHAPTER FIFTEEN

After establishing that the truth of Christ's resurrection was a vital part of the gospel which the apostles preached and the Corinthians believed, Paul argues that those who deny the bodily resurrection of believers virtually deny Christ's resurrection and empty the faith of its saving content [vv 1–19]. But now that Christ has been raised as the first-fruits of a new humanity, he has cancelled the curse we inherited from Adam, and ensured the certainty of our resurrection at his coming. Then, having subdued all his enemies, he shall deliver up the kingdom to his Father, that God may be all in all [vv 20–28]. If the Corinthians are right in their shameful denial of this truth, why are they so inconsistent as to practise baptism for the dead, and why does their apostle daily risk his life for the sake of the gospel? [vv 29–34]. Paul refutes the sceptical objections to the resurrection by showing that the relation which the glorified body sustains to our present body is one of vital continuity but not absolute identity, even as the seed that is sown bears no apparent relation to the form that God gives to the plant. So since God organizes matter in an infinite variety of ways, there is no reason to suppose that it is beyond his power to raise to eternal life the body that is sown in corruption. As we inherit our natural life from Adam, so we receive our spiritual life from Christ. And as we have borne the image of the earthy, so we shall bear the image of the heavenly. For flesh and blood cannot inherit the kingdom of God [vv 35–50]. This great change will take place at Christ's coming when the living will be transformed without experiencing death in the same moment that the dead are raised to glory. With this certainty set before them, Paul exhorts the Corinthians to be always abounding in the work of the Lord, because they know that they shall be so gloriously rewarded by him [vv 51–58].

Paul avoids a formal announcement of his last great subject because some in Corinth were disputing the truth of the Resurrection [v 12]. He adopts this course to ensure the unbiased attention of his readers as he thoroughly rehearses the vital facts of the gospel on which their faith rests [vv 1–11]. Presumably those who embraced this error were influenced by the Greek idea of the body (*sōma*) being the tomb (*sēma*) of the soul. And because they thought of death as liberating the immortal soul from the shackles of the earthly body, they 'looked for and desired no resurrection; and their formula, perhaps somewhat scoffingly and certainly somewhat magisterially pronounced, was: "There is no rising again of dead men" ' (Warfield). Unhappily, these deniers of the Resurrection are not without numerous successors today, including both the 'scholarly' or rationalistic and the 'spiritual' or mystical varieties of unbelief. Hence Paul's masterly treatment of this fundamental article of Christian belief is as much needed now as when it was first written.

*V*1: **Now I make known unto you, brethren, the gospel which I preached unto you, which also ye received, wherein also ye stand, *v* 2: by which also ye are saved, if ye hold fast the word which I preached unto you, except ye believed in vain.**

Paul gently rebukes the knowledgeable Corinthians by 'making known' to them the gospel which they had already accepted. It is the same gospel which he had preached to them, which they had received, in which they now stand, and through which they are being saved. This process began at the very moment when they believed the word Paul preached to them, but it will be consummated only if they continue to hold it fast (see note on 1:18).

I make known, I say, **with what word I preached it unto you, if ye hold it fast,** (RV margin) This is really an indirect question and it is the climax of the entire sentence. Paul had given the Corinthians a very precise statement of the gospel, and he supposes that they still hold fast this 'form of words' (Barrett), but his assumption can only be endorsed by their own affirmative response.

except ye believed in vain. Or rather 'without due consideration' (Arndt-Gingrich). Unless they had failed to lay hold of the promised blessings of the gospel by heedlessly rushing into a profession of it. Was his confidence in them ill-founded? Surely not! Paul expects them to say that the reality of their conversion is not open to doubt.

*V*3: **For I delivered unto you first of all that which also I received: that Christ died for our sins according to the scriptures;** *v* 4: **and that he was buried; and that he hath been raised on the third day according to the scriptures;** *v* 5: **and that he appeared to Cephas; then to the twelve;**

For I delivered to you as of first importance what I also received, (RSV) Paul passed on to the Corinthians the facts he had received from the eyewitnesses of the vital events of a certain Easter week. For though he is an apostle in virtue of his encounter with the Risen Lord, his knowledge of the earthly life of Jesus was conveyed to him by the testimony of the other apostles. Yet he speaks of this testimony as coming to him directly from the Lord (see note on 11:23). And this is because: '*Transmission by the apostles is not effected by men, but by Christ the Lord himself who thereby imparts this revelation.* All that the Church knows about the words of Jesus, about stories of his life, or about their interpretation, comes from the apostles. One has received this revelation, another that. The apostle is essentially one who passes on what he has received by revelation. But since everything has not been revealed to each individual apostle, each one must first pass on his testimony to another [Gal 1:18; 1 Cor 15:11], and only the entire *paradosis* (tradition), to which all the apostles contribute, constitutes the paradosis of Christ' (Oscar Cullmann, *The Early Church*, p. 73).

1. **that Christ died for our sins according to the scriptures;** Thus Paul is here clearly quoting a very early tradition, and though he does not actually refer to Christ as the Suffering Servant of God, he obviously sees the work of Christ as the fulfilment of *Is* 53 (so Oscar Cullmann, *The Christology of the New Testament*, pp. 76, 79). Since 'our sins' were the only reason for Christ's death, this means that he died for us sinners, as the substitutionary sacrifice through whom we receive the forgiveness of sins. 'In other words, there was no gospel known in the primitive church, or in any part of it, which had not this as its foundation – that God forgives our sins because Christ died for them' (James Denney, *Studies in Theology*, p. 104). [Cf *Rom* 3:24–26; 4:25; 2 *Cor* 5:21; *Gal* 1:4]

2. **and that he was buried;** That Christ was buried attests both the completeness of his death and the reality of his resurrection. In this indirect reference to the empty tomb, which undoubtedly formed part of the original tradition, 'we have a first indication that the risen Lord, as Paul preached him, possessed a body identical with that in which he had been buried, a body of flesh' (J. A. Schep).

3. and that he hath been raised on the third day according to the scriptures; For the second time it is asserted that these events were an exact fulfilment of the prophetic testimony of Scripture. With regard to the difficult phrase 'on the third day', it may be said that it was Christ himself who taught the scriptural necessity of his rising again on the third day [cf *Luke* 24:46; *Jonah* 1:17; *Matt* 12:40]. The death and burial of Jesus took place once for all, but having been raised from the dead he remains the Risen One in perpetuity. 'By death and burial he came down to our level, by resurrection he raised us to his' (Robertson – Plummer).

4. and that he appeared to Cephas; then to the twelve; The truth of the resurrection was confirmed by unimpeachable witnesses. Peter is placed first because he was the first apostle to see the Risen Lord [*Luke* 24:34]. Then he was seen by 'the twelve'. These words designate 'the college of the apostles, without exact regard to number: actually *ten*, wanting Judas Iscariot, and Thomas absent on the first meeting' (Findlay).

*V*6: **then he appeared to above five hundred brethren at once, of whom the greater part remain until now, but some are fallen asleep;**

Paul lays stress on the fact that Christ was seen by more than 500 brethren at once, and this meeting is almost certainly to be identified with that recorded in *Matt* 28:7, 10, 16. As he writes this letter some twenty years later, most of these witnesses are still able to confirm this testimony with their own lips, 'but some are fallen asleep'. This remarkable expression is not without its point in the argument. Because these men had faced death in the hope of the resurrection through faith in the Risen Christ, they could regard it as nothing more than a sleep [cf *Acts* 7:60]. 'If there was no resurrection in store for them, how strange was their lot!' (Robertson – Plummer).

*V*7: **then he appeared to James; then to all the apostles;**

Apart from this verse we should not know that James, the
Lord's half-brother [*Matt* 13:55], owed his conversion to a
special resurrection appearance [cf *John* 7:5]; a fact which explains the presence of 'his brethren' amongst the 120 disciples
at Jerusalem [*Acts* 1:14], and James' subsequent leadership of
the church there. Paul met James as well as Peter on his
first visit to the Jerusalem church [*Gal* 1:18f].

then to all the apostles; Since Paul presumably knew of the
absence of Thomas on the occasion mentioned in *v* 5, and his
consequent scepticism [*John* 20:24ff], he now distinctly says
'that *all* participated in this latter sight, which coincides in
point of time with *Acts* 1:6–12, not *John* 20:26. The witness
of the First Apostles to the resurrection was complete and
unqualified' (Findlay).

*V*8: **and last of all, as to the** *child* **untimely born, he
appeared to me also.**

Paul is overwhelmed by the thought of the grace manifested
to him 'last of all', *as* to one 'untimely born' in the family of
the apostles. 'As such a child, though born alive, is yet not
of the proper size, and scarcely worthy of the name of man,
so 'I am *the least* of the apostles', scarcely meet to be called
one; a supernumerary taken into the college out of regular
course; not led to Christ by gradual instruction, like a natural
birth, but by a sudden power, as those prematurely born'
(Fausset). Because the idea of a premature birth hardly fits
the words 'last of all', many reject this interpretation in
favour of the less likely notion that Paul is taking up an insult
hurled at him by his opponents (Arndt-Gingrich).

*V*9: **For I am the least of the apostles, that am not meet
to be called an apostle, because I persecuted the church
of God.**

Paul can never forget the shameful circumstances which accounted for his violent introduction to the apostolate. He regards himself as 'the least' of this highly favoured band, not in respect of his authority, but because he had been a persecutor of the people of God [1 *Tim* 1:13-15]. 'The forgiveness of sin does not obliterate the remembrance of it; neither does it remove the sense of unworthiness and ill-desert' (Hodge).

*V*10: **But by the grace of God I am what I am: and his grace which was bestowed upon me was not found vain; but I laboured more abundantly than they all: yet not I, but the grace of God which was with me.**

It was not by personal merit but by the grace of God that Paul became an apostle after being a persecutor. Nor was this grace bestowed upon him in vain, for he laboured more abundantly than all the rest of the apostles. This point was worth making to a community which was apt to compare him unfavourably with others. Moreover, he refers not simply to his toil but also to its results. For 'by his single labours Paul had extended the kingdom of Christ over a region wider than all the Twelve had traversed up to this date' (Findlay). Yet he does not say this to boast of his own achievements, but to magnify the grace of God without which all his work would have been to no purpose. 'Grace at once made him something and co-operated with him; in the words of the Tenth Article, grace 'prevents (i.e. anticipates) us that we may have a good will, and works with us when we have that good will' (Edwards). [cf *Phil* 2:12, 13]

*V*11: **Whether then** *it be* **I or they, so we preach, and so ye believed.**

After this personal digression [*vv* 9, 10], Paul sums up the paragraph in an emphatic statement of great importance.

Although *each* apostle had his own distinctive contribution to make to the gospel [*v* 3], they *all* preached the same gospel [*vv* 3–5], and this is the good news which *you* believed! Therefore any divergence from these basic beliefs of the gospel cuts a man off from all the blessings of the gospel. 'All the apostles agreed in this testimony; all Christians agree in the belief of it; by this faith they live, in this faith they die' (Matthew Henry).

*V*12: **Now if Christ is preached that he hath been raised from the dead, how say some among you that there is no resurrection of the dead?**

It is important to note that this argument is addressed to believers. The whole basis of its appeal lies in the Christian experience of the readers, and this is why it has nothing to say about the general resurrection of all men [*Dan*12:2]. Paul's line of reasoning here could not be applied to unbelievers: Because you are 'in Christ', you will rise as Christ rose from the dead.

Now if Christ is preached that he hath been raised from the dead, This remarkable expression shows that 'the preaching of Christ *is* the preaching *of his resurrection*' (Findlay). It is through the preaching of the apostolic gospel that the *living* Christ raises dead men to new life. No such power attends the preaching of those whose perverted preference for another 'gospel' leads them to present another 'Christ' [*Gal* 1:7].

how say some among you that there is no resurrection of the dead?
The effect of this unexpected question upon the Corinthians must have been like that of a bomb exploding in their midst! 'How could they deny that dead men rise, when Christ, who was a dead man, had risen?' (Warfield). C. K. Barrett

makes the likely surmise that the Corinthian error was the same as that of Hymenaeus and Philetus [2 *Tim* 2:18]. These 'gnostics' affirmed with some plausibility [*Col* 3:1-4] that the resurrection – which presumably they equated with their regeneration – was past already. But Paul rejects this 'spiritual' deviation from the gospel by insisting that the first resurrection unto eternal life necessarily involved the future resurrection of the body.

*V*13: **But if there is no resurrection of the dead, neither hath Christ been raised:** *v* 14: **and if Christ hath not been raised, then is our preaching vain, your faith also is vain.**

But if dead men do not rise, then it is impossible that Christ, who certainly died, can have risen from the dead. The argument involves the true and full humanity of the Lord, and the reassumption of his human body in the resurrection. Paul points out that if this supposition were true, then not only is the apostolic message devoid of reality, but also the faith that is founded upon it. 'Christianity becomes an unreal system of notions, like other phantoms of the theatre, if it is not an interpretation of facts. Faith also is no more faith; for faith must act on an external fact and a living person' (Edwards). [1 *Pet* 1:3]

*V*15: **Yea, and we are found false witnesses of God; because we witnessed of God that he raised up Christ: whom he raised not up, if so be that the dead are not raised.**

Moreover, in that case the apostles are discovered to be 'impostors of the worst kind, for their testimony bears on a false fact which they dared to ascribe to God himself!' (Godet). For they witnessed *against* God 'that he raised up Christ: whom he raised not up, if so be that the dead are not raised'. For Paul the matter at issue is quite simple: '"Either he rose from the grave, or we lied in affirming it" – the dilemma admits of no escape' (Findlay). There is no good news for mankind in the preaching of a myth!

*V*16: **For if the dead are not raised, neither hath Christ been raised: 17: and if Christ hath not been raised, your faith is vain; ye are yet in your sins.**

Paul restates the thought of *v* 13 in order to spell out the fatal consequences which lie hidden in the Corinthian denial of the resurrection. In *v* 14 he showed that this error emptied faith in Christ of all *reality*; in *v* 17 he emphasizes the complete *futility* of such a faith. 'If there is no resurrection, there is also no redemption, no reconciliation with God, no justification, no life and salvation. If Christ is still dead, then every believer is still dead in trespasses and sins. As long as Christ, our surety, is not released, it is certain that our debt is not paid, we are still liable, no matter how much we may trust in some supposed payment or in some release without payment' (Lenski). [*Rom* 4:24, 25]

*V*18: **Then they also that are fallen asleep in Christ have perished.**

This depicts the inevitably tragic result of believing what is not objectively true. If Christ was not raised from the dead, then faith in Christ is nothing more than a cruel delusion which will be shattered by the awful reality of death. 'There is a sharp contrast between the two terms: *falling asleep in Christ* and *having perished*. To close the eyes in the joy of salvation, to open them in the torments of perdition! The verb *apōlonto*, "perished", cannot designate annihilation, for it is explained by the preceding expression: "to be yet in sins". It denotes a state of perdition in which the soul remains under the weight of divine condemnation' (Godet).

*V*19: **If we have only hoped in Christ in this life, we are of all men most pitiable.**

If we have turned out to be no more than Christ-hopers and staked on that our whole present life, then we are of all men most pitiable. (Vos) Our plight is then most pitiable for two reasons. One is that unrealized hope 'is the most futile and ill-fated frustration of life-purpose'. The other is 'that when this futile hope so engrosses a man as to monopolize him for an unreal world such a state of mind involves the forfeit of all palpable realities of life, a sacrifice at bottom of all this-worldliness for another-worldliness that has no substance' (Vos).

*V*20: **But now hath Christ been raised from the dead, the firstfruits of them that are asleep.**

Paul has made explicit 'the hideous corollaries' which are implicit in the denial by 'some' [*v* 12] of 'the possibility of dead men rising' (Warfield). 'But now' is an expression often used by the apostle to introduce important statements [cf 13:13; *Rom* 3:21; 6:22; 7:6; *Col* 1:21], and this triumphant affirmation marks a glorious return to reality. Here he begins to speak of the consequences of Christ's resurrection for believers [*vv* 20–28]. Throughout the chapter his emphasis is consistently soteriological; he does not refer to God's judgment upon the unbelieving as being outside the scope of his present purpose [cf 2 *Thess* 1:8, 9]. For the Corinthians have not been appointed to wrath, but unto the obtaining of salvation through the Lord Jesus Christ [1 *Thess* 5:9].

In designating Christ as 'the firstfruits' Paul firmly puts the resurrection of Christ's people in the future, and thus contradicts the errorists who claim that the resurrection is past already (see note on *v* 12). The term 'implies community of nature with the "harvest" to follow; i.e. Christ's resurrection promises the ultimate home-gathering of all God's people. The full harvest was foreshadowed and consecrated by the first sheaf brought as an offering on the day following the sabbath after the Passover [*Lev* 23:10f], i.e. on Easter Day, the day of Christ's resurrection. Death with its sting gone [*v* 55] is for Christians no more than falling "asleep"' (Hillyer).

*V*21: **For since by man *came* death, by man *came* also the resurrection of the dead.** *V* 22: **For as in Adam all die, so also in Christ shall all be made alive.**

The italics show that there are no verbs, and the omission of the article before each noun stresses its quality. Since it was through man that mankind became mortal [*Rom* 5:12], through man also is resurrection from death [*Rom* 5:15, etc.]. This goes deeper than 'firstfruits' in that it points to Christ as the 'beginning', the very principle and root of resurrection-life [*Col* 1:18]. 'Through man' implies 'that Death is not, as philosophy supposed, a law of finite being or a necessity of fate; it is an event of history, a calamity brought by man upon himself and capable of removal by the like means' (Findlay).

In *v* 22 the second 'all' is not co-extensive with the first. It is true that there is no exception to the dying in Adam, but that is not Paul's point here; nor does he suggest that there is no exception to the being made alive in Christ. What he *does* mean to say is that as there is no dying outside of Adam, so there is no quickening apart from Christ. 'Both alike are heads of humanity. But they are unlike in this (as also in other things, *Rom* 5:15), that men are in Adam by nature, in Christ by faith' (Edwards). And just as it needed more than a 'mythical' Adam to produce the concrete reality of universal death, so it requires more than a 'mythical' resurrection of Christ to annul the power of death for all believers [cf *Rom* 6:5–11].

CHAPTER 15, VERSE 23

*V*23: **But each in his own order: Christ the firstfruits; then they that are Christ's, at his coming.**

G. Vos rightly maintains that the word *tagma* is not used here in the sense of 'division', 'troup', or 'group' as though several resurrections were involved, for the only point of comparison is that of 'order, sequence of occurrence'. Paul is affirming that in the order of the resurrection Christ as the 'firstfruits' necessarily precedes the final harvest. Probably it had been urged against the apostle's doctrine of the resurrection, that the resurrection of believers ought to take place immediately after their death. To this he replies: 'each in his own order'. Christ must come first because he is the source of the whole process, but the resurrection of his people awaits his return [cf *vv* 50–53].

*V*24: **Then *cometh* the end, when he shall deliver up the kingdom to God, even the Father; when he shall have abolished all rule and all authority and power.**

'The end' is *the end*! It is true that 'then' need not mean immediately; it could indicate the next significant event. But the two 'when' clauses which follow suggest that it should be taken to mean 'thereupon' (Barrett). Thus, 'the period between the two advents is the period of Christ's kingdom, and when He comes again it is not to institute His kingdom, but to lay it down [*vv* 24, 28]. The completion of His conquest, which is marked by conquering "the last enemy", death [*v* 26], which in turn is manifest when the just arise and Christ comes [*vv* 54, 23], marks also the end of His reign [*v* 25] and the delivery of the kingdom to God, even the Father [*v* 24]. This is indubitably Paul's assertion here, and it is in perfect harmony with the uniform representation of the New Testament, which everywhere places Christ's kingdom before and God's after the Second Advent' (B. B. Warfield, 'The Prophecies of St. Paul', *Biblical and Theological Studies*, p. 487).

when he shall have abolished all rule and all authority and power. It was at the cross that Christ won the decisive battle over these hostile powers which seek to oppose the fulfilment of God's saving purpose [*Col* 2:15; 1 *Pet* 3:22], and he continues the conflict against these enemies throughout his reign [*v* 25], until with the resurrection of his people the final victory is won in the war against sin and death.

*V*25: **For he must reign, till he hath put all his enemies under his feet.**

'Here the kingship of Christ is equivalent to the process of subjecting one enemy after another. After the last enemy, death, has been conquered, there is no further need for the kingdom of Christ: hence it is delivered up to God the Father. Christ's kingdom as a process of conquest precedes the final kingdom of God as a settled permanent state' (G. Vos, *The Kingdom and the Church*, p. 53) [*Ps* 110:1]

*V*26: **The last enemy that shall be abolished is death.**

Death, which is here personified, is the *last* of these enemies to be abolished or brought to nought. The verb is in the present tense and this denotes the certainty of its conquest [*vv* 53–57]. When Christ returns, his triumph 'over all powers hostile to God and over all that has come into the world through sin will be manifest, and that will mean the full liberation of the people of God from all the consequences of sin, also from temporal death, which means that the resurrection of the body will then take place' (Grosheide). [*v* 23]

*V*27: **For, He put all things in subjection, under his feet. But when he saith, All things are put in subjection, it is evident that he is excepted who did subject all things unto him.**

[224]

The final defeat of death, the last enemy, is made certain by the fact that God has put all things under the feet of Christ [*Ps* 8:6]. How this victory over death was achieved by the Lord is shown by the interpretation which is given of *Ps* 8:6 in *Heb* 2:6-18. But when God says in Scripture that he has subjected 'all things' to Christ as Mediator, it is evident that he did not include himself in this subjection. The purpose of the qualification is to prepare the Corinthians for Paul's final statement of what will take place at the end [*v* 28].

*V*28: **And when all things have been subjected unto him, then shall the Son also himself be subjected to him that did subject all things unto him, that God may be all in all.**

When the triumph of Christ the Son is at last complete, he will surrender his mediatorial kingship to the Father from whom he received it. It is clear that Christ cannot divest himself of that sovereignty which belongs to him as the eternal Son, and he will for ever remain the Head of the church which he has redeemed with his blood, but the final consummation of all things will bring his work as Mediator to an end. And this work comes to an *end* simply because the exercise of this office belongs to the *temporal* sphere; 'it is bound up with the subdual of this world, and it is this, therefore, when returned to the Father, that makes the glory of God complete' (Raymond O. Zorn, *Church and Kingdom*, p. 138).

that God may be all in all. The termination of the mediatorial office will bring to an end the Son's subordination to the Father in the economy of redemption in order that the one God (Father, Son, and Holy Spirit) may be all in all. From that moment onward 'the Triune God in all three persons conjointly, one God, shall stand supreme amid glorified humanity in the new heaven and the new earth' (Lenski). [*Rev* 21:3]

*V*29: **Else what shall they do that are baptized for the dead? If the dead are not raised at all, why then are they baptized for them?**

Paul abruptly turns from this apocalyptic vision of the future to show that the Corinthians' denial of the resurrection is inconsistent with a practice which presupposes a belief in it. For 'if the dead are not raised at all', then is it not the height of absurdity to baptize the living on behalf of the dead? 'The Greeks believed that the souls of the dead were benefited by the funeral honours paid to the body. This widespread feeling would find its way into the church and render the administration of a sacrament on behalf of the dead easy of introduction' (Edwards). Although Paul mentions this practice for the purpose of his argument, the phrase 'what shall *they* do' makes it evident that he is far from giving his approval to it. Moreover, as Hodge points out in his very helpful discussion of this notoriously difficult verse, the entire disappearance of the custom in the orthodox church 'is probably to be referred to the practice having been forbidden by the apostle as soon as he reached Corinth' [cf 11:34b].

*V*30: **why do we also stand in jeopardy every hour?**

Moreover, if there is no resurrection, there is no point in enduring hardship and braving danger for the sake of Christ. If the apostles' faith in this fundamental truth of the gospel were misplaced, then they were risking their lives for a dream without substance. They had lost hold of reality to embrace a mirage.

*V*31: **I protest by that glorying in you, brethren, which I have in Christ Jesus our Lord, I die daily.**

Paul dies daily because the preaching of the gospel exposes him to innumerable dangers [2 *Cor* 1:8, 9, 11:23]. This he solemnly affirms by the pride that he has in his brethren in Corinth. But though he glories in their faith, he returns all the credit for their conversion to Christ. 'This very name and title is full of the idea of the resurrection. Without the resurrection we should have no "Christ Jesus, our Lord", to commission Paul, to accomplish great things through Paul, to make the Corinthians Paul's glory, pride and joy' (Lenski).

*V*32: **If after the manner of men I fought with beasts at Ephesus, what doth it profit me? If the dead are not raised, let us eat and drink, for to-morrow we die.**

What would it avail me that, humanly speaking, I 'fought with wild beasts' at Ephesus? (Moffatt). Here Paul uses figurative language to recall a specific occasion during his stay at Ephesus when the violence of the opposition he encountered could be likened to fighting with wild beasts. Certainly from a human standpoint he could gain nothing by risking the speedy dissolution of his life *as man* in this way. 'Paul's point is that, if there is no resurrection, the dead cannot exist as men and that they consequently do not live in the full sense of the word' (Grosheide). [*Ps* 115:17]

If the dead are not raised, let us eat and drink, for to-morrow we die. This quotation of *Is* 22:13 LXX 'describes the reckless indulgence of the despisers of God's call to mourning, – Let us enjoy the good things of life now, for it soon will end. Paul imitates the language of sceptics, to reprove their theory and practice. "If men but persuade themselves that they should die like the beasts, they soon will live like beasts too." (*South*)' (Fausset).

*V*33: **Be not deceived: Evil companionships corrupt good morals.** Paul quotes the heathen poet Menander to convince the Corinthians of the danger of mixing pagan notions with the truth of the gospel. False teaching not only poisons the mind, but also demoralizes the life. 'The doubts of some in the Corinthian church concerning the resurrection of the dead was the consequence of their too intimate intercourse with their heathen neighbours' (Edwards).

*V*34: **Awake to soberness righteously, and sin not; for some have no knowledge of God: I speak *this* to move you to shame.**

Awake out of drunkenness righteously, (RV margin) 'A startling call, to men fallen as if into a drunken sleep under the seductions of sensualism and heathen society and the fumes of intellectual pride. "Righteously" signifies the *manner* of the awaking; it is *right* the Corinthians should rouse themselves from self-delusion; Paul assails their conscience' (Findlay).

and sin not; literally, 'and do not go on missing the mark'. Those who prefer independent thought to revealed truth miss the mark set by God for all our thinking. 'This is the worst kind of sinning, for it affects not only our conduct but corrupts the very heart, the source of all conduct' (Lenski). [*Prov* 4:23]

for some have no knowledge of God: I speak *this* to move you to shame. 'Some of you are cherishing that ignorance of God which belongs to the heathen; and while it is natural in them, it is a shame to Christians' (Edwards).

*V*35: **But some one will say, How are the dead raised? and with what manner of body do they come?**

The next aspect of the subject to receive the apostle's animated attention is the nature of the resurrection body [*vv* 35-49]. The 'gnostic' [cf *v* 12], whose Sadducean objections are here anticipated, is characterized by Godet as 'one of those sages whose whole spiritual stock consists in not knowing God [*v* 34]'.

How are the dead raised? and with what manner of body do they come? These are two distinct questions. The first 'intimates *the impossibility of the thing*, and is answered in *v* 36; the latter, *the inconceivability of the manner*, answered in *vv* 37ff. . . . The sceptics advance their second question to justify the first: they say, "The resurrection Paul preaches is absurd; how can any one imagine a new body rising out of the perished corpse – a body suitable to the deathless spirit?"' (Findlay).

*V*36: **Thou foolish one, that which thou thyself sowest is not quickened except it die:**

The objector is foolish because he is blind to the quickening power of God which is daily displayed before him in nature. To think that what is 'dead' cannot be raised 'is in flagrant contradiction to the facts of experience: "what thou sowest is not made alive except it have died". Death, so far from being an obstacle to quickening, is its very prerequisite' (Vos). [*John* 12:24]

*V*37: **and that which thou sowest, thou sowest not the body that shall be, but a bare grain, it may chance of wheat, or of some other kind;**

Paul deals at greater length with the second objection. The resurrection is not made impossible by the Corinthians' complete inability to visualize what the resurrection-body will be like. For without previous experience it would be equally impossible to anticipate the appearance of the mature plant from the bare grain that is sown, whether it be wheat or any other kind of seed. 'What right then has a man to argue from the impossibility of pre-vision and pre-imagination, to the presumptuous conclusion that the forthcoming of a new differently-shaped and differently-apparelled body is *a priori* an absurdity?' (Vos).

*V*38: **but God giveth it a body even as it pleased him, and to each seed a body of its own.**

The body that God now gives to each seed is in accordance with his creative decree [*Gen* 1:11f]. Thus the identity which exists between the various kinds of seeds and their resultant plants has been established by God and is not due to any 'necessary natural processes' (Grosheide). From this it is safe to infer that such a God will not be nonplussed by the need to provide a suitable body for the souls of the redeemed.

*V*39: **All flesh is not the same flesh: but there is one *flesh* of men, and another flesh of beasts, and another flesh of birds, and another of fishes.**

'If even here, where the general conditions of life are the same, we see such diversity in animal organizations, flesh and blood appearing in so many forms, why should it be assumed that the body hereafter must be the same cumbrous vehicle of the soul that it is now?' (Hodge).

*V*40: **There are also celestial bodies, and bodies terrestrial: but the glory of the celestial is one, and the *glory* of the terrestrial is another.**

There is also a *discernible* difference between the glory of bodies celestial and of bodies terrestrial, for as G. Vos notes, glory 'is primarily a term of outward manifestation'. If Paul had been speaking of 'angelic bodies' there would have been no difference to note because such beings are not discerned by human vision; the reference is to the heavenly bodies of sun, moon, and stars as the next verse makes perfectly plain. Nor need we suppose 'that the apostle ascribes life and sensation to them, after the manner of Philo. There is not a trace in the New Testament of the Greek notion that the stars are living creatures' (Edwards).

*V*41: **There is one glory of the sun, and another glory of the moon, and another glory of the stars; for one star differeth from another star in glory.**

Not only is there a vast difference between the glory of heavenly and earthly bodies, but there are also gradations in glory to be seen among the heavenly bodies themselves. Even so, the God who made all these discernible differences will not be found wanting in the capacity to change the believer's present body that it may be conformed to the body of Christ's glory [*Phil* 3:21].

*V*42a: **So also is the resurrection of the dead.**

'Here, strictly speaking, is the answer to the second question of *v* 35: *With what body?* Answer: with a body which, far from being the reappearance of the former, will have characteristics of an absolutely opposite kind' (Godet). Robertson and Plummer draw attention to the rhythmical parallelizing (as in Hebrew poetry) of Paul's utterance as he works towards the triumphant conclusion, especially *vv* 42-49 and *vv* 51-57.

*V*42b: **It is sown in corruption; it is raised in incorruption: *v* 43: it is sown in dishonour; it is raised in glory: it is sown in weakness; it is raised in power: *v* 44: it is sown a natural body; it is raised a spiritual body**

'Our *present life* is the seed-time [*Gal* 6:7ff], and our "mortal bodies" [*Rom* 8:10f] are in the germinal state, concluding with death [*v* 36], out of which a wholly different organism will spring' (Findlay). As it was through sin that the body became subject to *corruption*, *dishonour*, and *weakness*, so it is only through redemption from sin that it will attain to the *incorruption*, *glory*, and *power* of the post-resurrection state [*Rom* 6:23; 8:11–23; 2 *Cor* 13:4; *Phil* 3:21].

But with the fourth contrast between what is sown and raised, Paul reaches a new stage in the argument. It is because he is intent on showing that from the beginning God made provision for a higher kind of body, that he now advances from the contrast between the sinful body and the body restored by redemption to that between the creation-body ('natural' or 'psychical') and the resurrection-body ('spiritual' or 'pneumatic'). For though the body as created by God was sinless, and was not therefore characterized by corruption, dishonour, and weakness, it was nevertheless a *natural* body adapted to earthly conditions of life, and as such was unfit to be the eternal habitation of the *Spirit* [*vv* 44–49]. This adjective 'spiritual' does not denote a new substance, as though the resurrection-body consisted of 'spirit', and was therefore immaterial or ethereal. It rather points to a new *determination* or *origin*, for it is a body that is brought forth and determined by the divine, heavenly power (so Herman Ridderbos, *Paul*, p. 544).

*V*44b **If there is a natural body, there is also a spiritual body.**
*V*45: **So also it is written, The first man Adam became a living soul. The last Adam** *became* **a life-giving spirit.**

Paul argues that if one kind of body exists, then so does the other. He views the creation of the natural body as a necessary preparation for its perfection in glory, and finds support for this in Gen. 2:7. His interpretative addition of the words 'first' and 'Adam' emphasizes the preliminary character of God's work in creation. Paul's point is that apart from the entrance of sin into the world Adam needed to be changed.

He was immortal in that he was made in the moral image of God, but in the probationary state under which he was placed by God his body was not fitted for an immortal existence. 'Of this change in the constitution of his body, the tree of life was probably constituted the sacrament. For when he sinned, he was excluded from the garden of Eden, "lest he put forth his hand and take of the tree of life, and eat, and live for ever" [Gen 3:22]' (Hodge).

The last Adam _became_ a life-giving spirit. It is in the light of Christ's redemptive achievement that Paul is able to add his own antithesis to Gen 2:7 (so Bruce). It was when Christ's _body_ was raised and glorified that he became a life-giving _spirit_ [cf Rom 1:4; 8:11; 2 Cor 3:17]. For then, 'as the reward for his atoning death, He _received_ the promised Spirit in His resurrection and ascension [Matt 28:18; Acts 2:33]. He became a life-giving spirit as _the last Adam_, i.e., the last _man_: the unique and exclusive representative of those whom the Father gives Him [John 6:37, 17:9], who leads them to that glory which Adam should have obtained for the human race as its first representative [Rom 5:12ff; 1 Cor 15:20ff, 49)' (J. A. Schep, _The Nature of the Resurrection Body_, p. 176).

V46: Howbeit that is not first which is spiritual, but that which is natural; then that which is spiritual.

Paul probably had a polemical purpose in making this emphatic assertion, because he reverses the order envisaged by Philo, who held that the ideal, heavenly man was prior to Adam, the earthly and material copy. Accordingly, he insists that the natural man precedes the spiritual man, who is not an archetypal heavenly man but the second man _from heaven_ [v 47]. The reference is not therefore to the pre-existence of Christ, but to that future coming of Christ by which all his people shall be changed [vv 50ff; Phil 3:21].

*V*47: **The first man is of the earth, earthy: the second man is of heaven.**

'As *earthy* man is differentiated from what the risen Christ already is and what man will one day be through Him' (E. Schweizer, *TDNT*, Vol. IX, p. 478). The real origin of Paul's doctrine of the second man from heaven is not Hellenistic but Jewish. For though he never uses the term Son of Man, his teaching here appears to be based on the Lord's own interpretation of *Dan* 7:13 [cf *Mark* 13:26; 14:62]. Thus Christ coming 'with the clouds of heaven' is seen as the climactic event which will perfect the salvation of his people and usher in the eternal state of glory [*v* 23; *Rom* 8:23; 1 *Thess* 4:16; 2 *Thess* 1:7].

*V*48: **As is the earthy, such are they also that are earthy: and as is the heavenly, such are they also that are heavenly.**

The comparison is simple when it is remembered that 'bodies' is the main theme of the paragraph (Barrett). All Adam's descendants are of the earth earthy [*v* 47], but at the resurrection those who belong to Christ – the second man from heaven – will then bear his image [*v* 49]. The parallel of *v* 45 breaks down here, for though man is a 'living soul' like Adam, he will never be a 'life-giving' Creator Spirit like Christ. He will only be a 'spiritual body' (so E. Schweizer, *TDNT*, Vol. 9, p. 663).

*V*49: **And as we have borne the image of the earthy, we shall also bear the image of the heavenly.**

Although there is a variant reading, 'let us bear', the future tense, 'we shall bear', expresses the certainty of the event and is demanded by the context. At present we are forced to live on in a corruptible body, but as F. F. Bruce observes, at the resurrection the Creator's purpose that man should reflect his image [*Gen* 1:26], will be finally realized when we are conformed to the Man who is himself the image of God [cf *Rom* 8:29; 2 *Cor* 4:4].

*V*50: **Now this I say, brethren, that flesh and blood cannot inherit the kingdom of God; neither doth corruption inherit incorruption.**

What Paul now asserts sums up what he has said about the natural body in the previous verses [*vv* 44–49]. Such a natural body of 'flesh and blood' *cannot* inherit the kingdom of God because it is evident that the corruptible *does not* inherit incorruption. Hence the present constitution of the body must be changed before it is fit to enter that kingdom in which matter is no longer governed by the soul, but is ruled by the Spirit. The sequel shows that Paul is far from denying the material nature of the resurrection-body; 'our flesh will share in the glory of God, but only after it has been renewed and restored to life by the Spirit of Christ' (Calvin). [cf *Luke* 24:39]

*V*51: **Behold, I tell you a mystery: We all shall not sleep, but we shall all be changed,** *v* 52: **in a moment, in the twinkling of an eye, at the last trump: for the trumpet shall sound, and the dead shall be raised incorruptible, and we shall be changed.**

Paul's exclamation 'Behold' draws the attention of the Corinthians to his revelation of a hitherto undisclosed mystery: it is that the bodies of all believers shall be changed, whether they happen to be dead or alive at Christ's coming. Behind the passive verb 'stands the almighty agent who shall work this miraculous change' (Lenski). Many restrict the pronoun 'we' to Paul and his readers, and gratuitously assume that the apostle expected to be alive at the Parousia, but the reference is general and includes the whole church, i.e. all Christians.

This change will be all but instantaneous, taking place in 'the twinkling of an eye, at the last trump'. The sound of that trumpet at the moment pre-determined by God will mark the end of the present age, and consummate the salvation of his people, for then the dead shall be raised incorruptible, and the living shall be changed. As Warfield well says, 'Truly events stay not, when the Lord comes'. [cf 1 Thess 4:13-17]

V53: **For this corruptible must put on incorruption, and this mortal must put on immortality.**

This gives the reason why we must be changed. 'It is impossible that corruption should inherit incorruption. This reason applies equally to the quick [living] and to the dead. With regard to both classes it is true that these vile bodies must be fashioned like unto Christ's glorious body' (Hodge). [cf 2 Cor 5:1-4]

V54: **But when this corruptible shall have put on incorruption, and this mortal shall have put on immortality, then shall come to pass the saying that is written, Death is swallowed up in victory.**

But when . . . then The resurrection will mark the final 'overthrow of the King of Terrors' (Findlay). This clothing of the saints with immortality will be the fulfilment of 'the farthest reaching of all Old Testament prophecies' [Is 25:8], since it reverses the sentence of doom that was pronounced in Gen 3 (A. Dillmann). 'The Scriptures announce how one death (Christ's) devoured the others (ours)' (Luther).

V55: **O death, where is thy victory? O death, where is thy sting?**

The apostle's exultant shout of triumph is a free adaptation of the language of *Hosea* 13:14. In that day the illusory nature of death's victory will be apparent to all; then its venomous sting will be abolished for ever. T. C. Edwards interestingly notes that Paul never used the word Hades, and that his substitution of Death for it in this passage can hardly have been accidental. For though the grave now claims the *bodies* of believers, their *souls* never enter the shadowy underworld of Hades.[1]

*V*56: **The sting of death is sin; and the power of sin is the law:**

As sin's lethal sting introduced the universal reign of death, so its condemning power is derived from the law of God. If man had not sinned, he had not died [*Gen* 2:17; *Rom* 5:12]. Death therefore maintains itself in the sin which calls for condemnation, and in the law which passes sentence upon all who violate its divine sanctions [*Rom* 7:7ff]. This means 'that victory over sin is possible only through the propitiation, which is Jesus Christ [cf *Rom* 3:25]. The headship of the second Man has no real existence apart from his atonement. Christ acts as a quickening spirit through redemption. In this way the apostle connects the resurrection of believers with the death of Christ as well as with the power of his heavenly life. Thus to make the judicial intent of Christ's death the key-stone of the discussion is an unmistakable sign of Pauline thought' (Edwards).

*V*57: **but thanks be to God, who giveth us the victory through our Lord Jesus Christ.**

This objective atonement produces subjective results in the lives of all believers. What has been gained for us by Christ is

1. On the modernist construction of Sheol-Hades see the very fine discussion by L. Berkhof in his *Systematic Theology*, pp. 681–686.

daily being given to us by God [cf *Rom* 8:37]. Paul's use of the present tense does not denote the certainty of the future resurrection, but expresses the assurance that even now we have forgiveness of sins. 'If the sting of death is sin, victory over death must be forgiveness of the sin. . .The apostle's purpose is to encourage timid Christians in the conflict against sin with the certain hope of victory at last' (Edwards).

*V*58: **Wherefore, my beloved brethren, be ye steadfast, unmovable, always abounding in the work of the Lord, forasmuch as ye know that your labour is not vain in the Lord.**

Wherefore, Paul here concludes his great doctrinal argument on a very practical note: it is that the certainty of the resurrection must encourage diligence in present duty. The apostle's method of instruction teaches us that as no exhortation is in place without doctrine, so no exposition of doctrine is complete without exhortation.

my beloved brethren, Despite his severe reproofs, Paul assures the Corinthians that his affection for them remains undiminished.

be ye steadfast, unmovable, They are to resist the seductive power of unbelief which would overthrow their faith in the doctrine of the resurrection. 'It is implied that an attempt of the kind has been intentionally made in the Corinthian church. Cf. *vv* 32–34' (Edwards) [2 *Cor* 11:2, 3]

always abounding in the work of the Lord, 'There is perhaps an implied correction of their disproportionate activity in speculation, cf 1:18f. "The work of the Lord" is preparation for the end, in mutual service and the spread of the Gospel: and the end has been made sure by the resurrection of the Lord' (St. John Parry).

forasmuch as ye know that your labour is not in vain in the Lord. It is because their work is in the Lord that it is not an *empty* expenditure of energy: 'this is not an activity of external demonstration, wrought in vacuity, as earthly labour so often is, but serious toil wrought in the sphere of eternal reality. This is why Paul also uses the present *is*, and not the future *will be*' (Godet).

CHAPTER SIXTEEN

In the last chapter Paul deals with various practical and personal matters. He first gives directions concerning the collection for impoverished fellow-believers at Jerusalem [vv 1–4]. He then speaks of his travel plans which include a projected visit to Corinth [vv 5–9]. Meanwhile he urges them to receive Timothy, and informs them that Apollos will not be visiting the church at this time [vv 10 12]. In his final exhortation to the congregation, Paul expresses his joy in receiving the delegates from Corinth, and sends the greetings of the believers in Asia [vv 13–20]. After adding his own greetings, the apostle pronounces a solemn anathema on anyone who does not love the Lord, and concludes with the benediction and an assurance of his love for them all [vv 21–24].

V1: **Now concerning the collection for the saints, as I gave order to the churches of Galatia, so also do ye.**

That Paul was no impractical visionary is shown by his rapid descent from the sublime truth of the resurrection to the mundane details of church administration. The familiar introductory formula, 'Now concerning', suggests that the collection was another matter on which the Corinthians had requested further guidance. In giving them the same direction that he gave to the churches of Galatia, Paul lets them know that they are not the only Gentiles who are asked to contribute to the support of the poor saints in Jerusalem. 'He proposes the Galatians as an example to the Corinthians, the Corinthians to the Macedonians, the Corinthians and the Macedonians to the Romans; 2 *Cor* 9:2; *Rom* 15:26. There is great force in examples' (Bengel). Persecution by unbelieving Jews and protracted periods of famine probably account for the dire straits to which these Jewish Christians were reduced. Paul regarded this collection as nothing less than the payment of a debt of gratitude [cf *Rom* 15:27]. He also felt that it would 'strikingly demonstrate the solidarity of the Gentile churches with the mother church, and do much to promote unity' (Morris).

*V*2: **Upon the first day of the week let each one of you lay by him in store, as he may prosper, that no collections be made when I come.**

Upon the first day of the week, This renders it certain 'that that day was already regarded by all Christians as a sacred day, and, as such, the proper day (as we find from *Acts* 20:7) for public worship. In this view, their laying by their weekly sum *on that day* would both stamp the contribution with a sacred character and hallow and stimulate the generous principle itself' (Brown).

let each one of you lay by him in store, 'Paul trusts the Corinthians: he does not ask them to hand in their collection on a weekly basis, they are allowed to keep the collected money and thus little by little a sufficient amount will be saved up' (Grosheide). [*Matt* 6:19-21; *Luke* 12:21]

as he may prosper, 'Paul makes the measure of God's blessing to us the measure of our return to him. . .At no time does he propose the old Jewish system of tithing to the churches under his care. The only references to tithes found in the New Testament take us back into the Old Testament,

Heb 5:7-9, or criticize the Pharisees at Christ's time, *Matt* 23:23; *Luke* 11:42, 18:12. This is quite decisive for us' (Lenski).

that no collections be made when I come. 'Paul would avoid the unseemliness and the difficulty of raising money suddenly, at the last moment; and he wishes when he comes to be free to devote himself to higher matters [cf *Acts* 6:2]' (Findlay).

*V*3 : **And when I arrive, whomsoever ye shall approve, them will I send with letters to carry your bounty unto Jerusalem: 4: and if it be meet for me to go also, they shall go with me.**

Paul wisely avoids handling the fund himself so that the Corinthians are given no opportunity to question his integrity [cf 1 *Thess* 2:5]. They are to appoint trustworthy men to deliver their gift, and he will authorize their mission by supplying them with 'letters' (written credentials) addressed to the leaders of the Jerusalem church.

If it seems advisable that I should go also, (RSV) This rendering is preferable, for the verse 'does not mean: if the collection is large enough I myself shall go with the delegation, but rather: if circumstances are such that the mission work demands my journeying to Jerusalem they shall go with me. Then letters will not be needed' (Grosheide).

*V*5 : **But I will come unto you, when I shall have passed through Macedonia; for I pass through Macedonia; 6: but with you it may be that I shall abide, or even winter, that ye may set me forward on my journey whithersoever I go. 7: For I do not wish to see you now by the way; for I hope to tarry a while with you, if the Lord permit.**

Paul writes from Ephesus of his future plans. It appears from 2 *Cor* 1:15, 16 that his original intention, presumably announced in the 'lost' letter [5:9], had been to visit them on his way and again on his return from Macedonia. But now he has decided that instead of paying them two flying visits, he will not call at Corinth on his way to Macedonia, because he *prefers* to stay longer with them on his return from Macedonia. This will give him the opportunity of dealing with their problems, and it will give them the privilege of helping him forward on his next journey, wherever that may take him. Thus Paul defers his visit, not from any lack of interest, but rather that he may be able to minister more effectively to them. Yet though this is his settled aim (which was in fact carried out, *Acts* 20:3), they must realize that all his plans are made in subjection to the will of the Lord [*Jas* 4:15].

*V*8: **But I will tarry at Ephesus until Pentecost; 9: for a great door and effectual is opened unto me, and there are many adversaries.**

Paul cannot come to them now because his work in Ephesus is not yet finished. At present he must remain in that city not only to grasp the great opportunities he has for effectively preaching the gospel [2 *Cor* 2:12; *Col* 4:3], but also to counter the fierce opposition which the signal success of his mission has aroused [*Acts* 19:9, 13f]. 'Great success in the work of the gospel commonly creates many enemies. The devil opposes the most, and makes them most trouble, who most heartily and successfully set themselves to destroy his kingdom' (Matthew Henry).

*V*10: **Now if Timothy come, see that he be with you without fear; for he worketh the work of the Lord, as I also do: 11: let no man therefore despise him.**

[243]

But set him forward on his journey in peace, that he may come unto me: for I expect him with the brethren.

Since Paul would send this letter by the shortest route, it would reach Corinth before Timothy [4:17], who was to come via Macedonia [*Acts* 19:22]. The somewhat strange request, to ensure that Timothy may stay with them 'without fear', suggests that Paul is afraid that after hearing eloquent preachers like Apollos they may be inclined to belittle this shy and diffident young man [cf 2 *Tim* 1:7]. Let them then realize that he is working faithfully alongside Paul in the same work for the Lord. Hence no one in Corinth is to despise Timothy. They are to receive him with respect and to send him on his way in peace, for Paul will eagerly await his return with the brethren whom he is now sending to Corinth with this letter (probably Titus and the 'brother' of 2 *Cor* 12:18).

*V*12: **But as touching Apollos the brother, I besought him much to come unto you with the brethren: and it was not at all *his* will to come now; but he will come when he shall have opportunity.**

Apparently the Corinthians had requested another visit from Apollos, but he refused to accept the invitation even though Paul had urged him to return with the brethren [*v* 11]. 'Considering the way in which Apollos had been made a rival to Paul in Corinth, it shows magnanimity on Paul's side to desire his return, and a modest delicacy on the side of Apollos to decline the request' (Findlay). [1:12]

*V*13: **Watch ye, stand fast in the faith, quit you like men, be strong. *V* 14: Let all that ye do be done in love.**

With these five imperatives Paul gathers up the burden of his message as he urges the Corinthians to develop the qualities in which they were sadly deficient. 1. The exhortation to watchfulness is directed against their heedlessness and recalls 15:33f. 2. The summons to stand fast in the faith rebukes their fickleness and this sums up such passages as 4:17, 10:12, 15:2, 11ff. 3. To play the man means that they must give up their childishness, especially as this relates to the question of spiritual gifts, cf 13:11; 14:20. 4. 'Be strong' was an appropriate word to those enfeebled by their compromises with paganism, cf ch 10. 5. Finally, the demand that all things be done in love again touches upon the radical fault of this community, cf chs 8 and 13.

*V*15: **Now I beseech you, brethren (ye know the house of Stephanas, that it is the firstfruits of Achaia, and that they have set themselves to minister unto the saints),** *v* 16: **that ye also be in subjection unto such, and to every one that helpeth in the work and laboureth.**

It is not because Stephanas and his household are the first to believe the gospel in the province that Paul calls them 'the firstfruits of Achaia', for some were converted through his preaching in Athens [*Acts* 17:34]. But to his mind 'the pledge of a future church came not in Athens, but in Corinth' with the conversion of a whole family (Edwards). Paul singles out this family as worthy of the Corinthians' respect and imitation because their forwardness in service happily matched the priority of their conversion.

'This respectful deference ought to be extended to every one who voluntarily makes himself like those of whom Paul has just spoken; their fellow-labourer by working for the good of the church. . .It is plain from this exhortation that the Corinthians were naturally prone to be lacking in submission and respect to those whom their age, experience, and services naturally pointed out for the veneration of the flock' (Godet).

*V*17: **And I rejoice at the coming of Stephanas and Fortunatus and Achaicus: for that which was lacking on your part they supplied.**

*V*18: **For they refreshed my spirit and yours: acknowledge ye therefore them that are such.**

Paul rejoices in the coming of these messengers from Corinth, for 'the lack of your own presence has been supplied by theirs as your deputies' (Brown). This had refreshed Paul's spirit, because the arrival of a delegation, presumably with a letter from the church, showed that the Corinthians, whatever their failings, still acknowledged his authority. Moreover, their own account of the situation in Corinth was not uniformly depressing, but also had its brighter side [1:4f]. In making this fraternal contact with Paul these men minister the same refreshment to the Corinthians. The apostle thus 'credits them with solicitous feelings that are just like his own' (Lenski). Therefore loyal service like theirs should compel the Corinthians gratefully to recognise the true worth of such men!

*V*19: **The churches of Asia salute you. Aquila and Prisca salute you much in the Lord, with the church that is in their house.**

All the churches of proconsular Asia send Christian greetings, to which their old friends Aquila and Prisca [*Acts* 18:2, 3], now with Paul in Ephesus [*Acts* 18:18], add special salutations in the Lord, together with the church that gathers in their house. 'As the same expression is used in *Rom* 16:5, in connection with their names, it is probable that both at Rome and Ephesus, they opened their house as a regular place of meeting for Christians. Their occupation as tent-makers probably required spacious apartments, suited for the purpose of such assemblies' (Hodge).

*V*20: **All the brethren salute you. Salute one another with a holy kiss.**

Finally, all the brethren at Ephesus salute their fellow-believers at Corinth, whom Paul here urges to salute one another with a holy kiss [cf *Rom* 16:16; 2 *Cor* 13:12; 1 *Thess* 5:26]. By doing this after having heard Paul's epistle, the Corinthians 'would indicate that they were united with one another and also with the churches of Asia' (Grosheide).

*V*21: **The salutation of me Paul with mine own hand.**

Paul has finished dictating his letter. It is now time for him to take the pen in his own hand, and write out the last few words himself [*vv* 21–24]. [cf 2 *Thess* 3:17] It is a moment charged with deep emotion, and Paul wishes to evoke a corresponding response in the hearts of his beloved Corinthians.

*V*22: **If any man loveth not the Lord, let him be anathema. Marana tha.**

This would come as a complete surprise and must have produced a profound feeling of shock when it was first read out in church [cf *Gal* 1:8, 9]. Truly Paul's letters are powerful! Here he deliberately uses the weaker word for love [*phileo*: cf *John* 21: 15–17] to stigmatize the *heartlessness* of those in whom even human affection for the Lord is wanting. He pronounces his solemn curse upon all who feign a love they do not feel for Christ. 'It is a *spurious* love that is accursed – a cold, false heart which, knowing the Lord, does not really love him' (Findlay).

Marana tha These two Aramaic words mean, 'Our Lord, come!' [cf *Rev* 22:20], and their preservation in a letter addressed to Greek-speaking Christians is 'the Achilles' heel' (A. E. J. Rawlinson) of the fantastic notion that the title

[247]

'Lord' was the invention of Hellenistic Christianity (advocated by W. Bousset and R. Bultmann). K. G. Kuhn points out that the untranslated Aramaic term is meaningful only if it was a fixed formula that was well-known in the churches. This means that its origin must be sought only in the Palestinian community, and that it had an important place in the worship of this community. The term is thus 'an important and authentic witness to the faith of the primitive Palestinian community. This confessed Jesus, the exalted Christ, as its Lord. It spoke of Him and prayed to Him as "our Lord". Here then, is the origin of the ascription of the name "Lord", the title *kurios*, to Jesus – a title which in Paul especially takes on profound and comprehensive significance in opposition to the *lords* of the Hellenistic world' (*TDNT*, Vol. IV, p. 470). (cf 8:5)

*V*23: **The grace of the Lord Jesus Christ be with you.**

'The apostle will not end with a word of warning or severity, but adds the usual benediction. Like a true teacher, as Chrysostom says, he helps not only with counsels, but with prayers' (Robertson – Plummer).

*V*24: **My love be with you all in Christ Jesus. Amen.**

Here the 'Amen' has been added by a later hand. It is a liturgical addition to the text [cf NIV). This is of some importance because its omission makes Paul's last words all the more impressive. For though Paul has found it necessary to administer severe reproofs, in closing he assures the Corinthians that even these were prompted by his love for them 'in Christ Jesus'. 'The last word that is and can be said – in Christ Jesus, in whom both you and I live and are one. It is the ground of the whole Epistle' (St. John Parry).

Soli Deo Gloria

BIBLIOGRAPHY AND ACKNOWLEDGEMENTS

The author expresses his grateful thanks to the following authors and publishers who have kindly given permission to reproduce quotations from their copyright works.

Barrett, C. K., *The First Epistle to the Corinthians* (BNTC) (A & C Black, 1971)

Boettner, Loraine, *Roman Catholicism* (Banner of Truth, 1966)

Bornkamm, Günther, *Early Christian Experience* (translated by Paul L. Hammer) (Harper & Row, 1969)

Bruce, F. F., *1 and 2 Corinthians* (NCB) (Oliphants, 1971)

Calvin, John, *The First Epistle of Paul the Apostle to the Corinthians* (translated by John W. Fraser) (Oliver and Boyd, 1960)

Chantry, Walter J., *Signs of the Apostles* (Banner of Truth, 1976)

Clark, Gordon H., *1 Corinthians – A Contemporary Commentary* (Presbyterian & Reformed, 1975)

Cullmann, Oscar, *The Early Church* (Edited by A. J. B. Higgins) (SCM 1956)

Douglas, J. D., Editor, *The New Bible Dictionary* (IVF, 1962)

Dunn, James, D. G., *Jesus and the Spirit* (SCM, 1975)

Edwards, T. C., *A Commentary on the First Epistle to the Corinthians* (Hodder & Stoughton, 1885)

Geldenhuys, Norval, *Supreme Authority* (Marshall, Morgan and Scott, 1953)

Grosheide, F. W., *Commentary on 1 Corinthians* (NLC) (Marshall, Morgan & Scott, 1954)

BIBLIOGRAPHY

Héring, Jean, *The First Epistle of Saint Paul to the Corinthians* (translated by A. W. Heathcote and P. J. Allcock) (Epworth, 1962)

Hillyer, Norman, *Commentary on 1 Corinthians* (NBC Revised) (IVP, 1970)

Kittel, G. and Friedrich, G., *Theological Dictionary of the New Testament* Vols. I–X translated by Geoffrey W. Bromiley: index by Ronald E. Pitkin) (Eerdmans, 1964–1976)

Lenski, R. C. H., *The Interpretation of 1 Corinthians* (Augsburg, 1961)

Mare, W. Harold, *1 Corinthians* (EBC) (Pickering & Inglis, 1976)

Martin, Ralph P., *Worship in the Early Church* (Marshall, Morgan & Scott, 1964)

Morris, Leon, *1 Corinthians* (TNTC) (Tyndale, 1958)

Morris, Leon, *The Apostolic Preaching of the Cross* (Tyndale, 1965)

Morris, Leon, *Spirit of the Living God* (IVP, 1969)

Moule, C. F. D., *An Idiom-Book of New Testament Greek* (CUP, 1968)

Murray, John *Principles of Conduct* (Tyndale, 1957)

Murray, John (contributor to), *The Infallible Word* (Presbyterian & Reformed, 1946)

Parry, R. St. John, *The First Epistle of Paul the Apostle to the Corinthians* (CGT) (CUP, 1916)

Robertson, A. T., *Word Pictures in the New Testament, Vol. IV* (Broadman, 1931)

Robertson, A. and Plummer, A., *Commentary on 1 Corinthians* (ICC) (T & T Clark, 1967)

Schep, J. A., *The Nature of the Resurrection Body* (Eerdmans, 1964)

Stonehouse, Ned B., *Paul before the Areopagus* (Tyndale, 1957)

Stott, John, *Baptism and Fullness* (IVP 1975)

Vine, W. E., *Expository Dictionary of New Testament Words* (Oliphants, 1958)

Vos, Geerhardus, *The Pauline Eschatology* (Eerdmans 1961)

Zorn, Raymond O., *Church and Kingdom* (Presbyterian and Reformed, 1962)

In addition to these, the following books were consulted:

Alford, Henry, *The Greek Testament* (Rivingtons, 1877)

Arndt, W. F. and Gingrich, F. W., *A Greek-English Lexicon of the New Testament* (University of Chicago Press, 1957)

Bengel, J. A., *New Testament Word Studies, Vol. 2* (Kregel, 1971)

Berkhof, L., *Systematic Theology* (Banner of Truth, 1959)

Bolton, Samuel, *The True Bounds of Christian Freedom* (Banner of Truth, 1964)

Brown, David, *1 Corinthians* (Popular Commentary on NT) (T & T Clark)

Bruner, F. D., *A Theology of the Holy Spirit* (Hodder & Stoughton, 1970)

Burgess, Anthony, *A Practical Commentary* on 1 Corinthians 3 (London, 1659)

Conzelmann, Hans, *1 Corinthians* (Hermeneia) (translated by James W. Leitch) (Fortress Press, 1975)

Craig, Clarence T., *The First Epistle to the Corinthians* (IB) (Abingdon, 1953)

Cullmann, Oscar, *The Christology of the New Testament* (translated by Shirley C. Guthrie and Charles A. M. Hall) (SCM, 1963)

Cullmann, Oscar, *Christ and Time* (translated by Floyd V. Filson) (SCM, 1971)

Davies, W. D., *Paul and Rabbinic Judaism* (SPCK, 1970)

Denney, James, *Studies in Theology* (Hodder & Stoughton, 1895)

Eadie, John, *Commentary on the Epistle to the Ephesians* (Zondervan reprint of 1883 ed.)

Edwards, Jonathan, *Charity and its Fruits* (Banner of Truth, 1969)

Fausset, A. R., *Commentary on 1 Corinthians* (JFB) (Collins, 1874)

Findlay, G. G., *Commentary on 1 Corinthians* (EGT) (Eerdmans, 1974)

Godet, F., *Commentary on 1 Corinthians* (T & T Clark 1886)

Henry, Matthew, *Commentary on the Holy Bible* (various editions)

Hodge, Charles, *Commentary on 1 Corinthians* (Banner of Truth, 1958)

Kennedy, H. A. A., *St. Paul and the Mystery-Religions* (Hodder & Stoughton, 1913)

Ladd, George Eldon, *A Theology of the New Testament* (Eerdmans, 1974)

Lightfoot, J. B., *Notes on the Epistles of St Paul* (Zondervan, 1957)

Lightfoot, J. B., *St. Paul's Epistle to the Philippians* (Zondervan, 1953)

Lloyd-Jones, D. M., *Conversions: Psychological and Spiritual* (IVF, 1963)

BIBLIOGRAPHY

Machen, J. G., *The Origin of Paul's Religion* (Eerdmans, 1965)

McKelvey, R. J., *The New Temple* (OUP, 1969)

Moffatt, James, *The First Epistle of Paul to the Corinthians* (MNTC) (Hodder & Stoughton, 1938)

Murray, John, *The Collected Writings*, Vol. 1 (Banner of Truth, 1976)

Owen, John, *Works*, Vol. 3 (Banner of Truth, 1966)

Poole, Matthew, *Commentary on the Holy Bible*, Vol. 3 (Banner of Truth, 1963)

Rawlinson, A. E. J., *The New Testament Doctrine of the Christ* (Longmans, Green, 1929)

Ridderbos, Herman (contributor to), *Revelation and the Bible* (Tyndale, 1959)

Ridderbos, Herman, *Paul – An Outline of His Theology* (translated by John Richard De Witt) (Eerdmans, 1975)

Robertson, A. T., *A Grammar of the Greek New Testament* (Broadman, 1934)

Ruef, John, *Paul's First Letter to Corinth* (PNTC) (Penguin, 1971)

Schweizer, Eduard, *The Church as the Body of Christ* (SPCK, 1965)

Shedd, W. G. T., *Sermons to the Spiritual Man* (Banner of Truth, 1972)

Smeaton, George, *The Apostles' Doctrine of the Atonement* (Zondervan, 1957)

Souter, Alexander, *A Pocket Lexicon of the Greek New Testament* (OUP, 1956)

Thrall, Margaret E., *1 & 2 Corinthians* (CBC) (CUP, 1965)

Trapp, John, *Commentary on the New Testament* (Sovereign Grace Book Club, 1958)

Vincent, Marvin R., *Word Studies in the New Testament* (Macdonald, n.d.)

Vos, Geerhardus, *The Kingdom and the Church* (Eerdmans, 1958)

Warfield, B. B., *Biblical and Theological Studies* (Presbyterian & Reformed, 1952)

Warfield, B. B., *Counterfeit Miracles* (Banner of Truth, 1972)

Warfield, B. B., *Faith and Life* (Banner of Truth, 1974)

Warfield, B. B., *The Lord of Glory* (Evangelical Press, 1974)

Warfield, B. B., *The Saviour of the World* (Mack Publishing, 1972)

Watson, T. E., *Baptism Not for Infants* (Watson, 1962)

Wiles, Gordon P., *Paul's Intercessory Prayers* (CUP, 1974)